Your Seat is at the End

Margaret Prosser
with Greg Watts

Your Seat is at the End
My Story

Margaret Prosser
with Greg Watts

Feather Duster Publications,
69 Witley Court,
Coram St.,
London,
WC1N 1HD

Cover photographs courtesy of TUC Library Collections,
London Metropolitan University and Wandsworth Heritage
Service.

ISBN 978-0-9572990-0-9

Contents

Acknowledgements

I would like to thank my children Jeffrey, Carol and Stella for being such stalwart supporters; Colin Roberts, who gave me the confidence to move on and up; Ray Collins, for being my best friend in the T&G; Bill Morris for his real understanding of and belief in equalities; and all the trade union women who continue the good fight. I would also like to thank Greg Watts for encouraging and helping me to write my story.

Foreword

MARGARET WAS ONE of the most remarkable people I came across in politics. Often, when I am asked about great people I have met and about those who were an inspiration for me, the anticipated answer is usually some world leader. However, it is more often the case that the most inspirational people are those behind the headlines, people with extraordinary life stories, people who overcame all the odds and did brilliantly despite it all. Margaret is such a person. She started life in the most unpromising way, married young to a partner who became severely disabled, and having to fight every inch of the way to get qualified, to bring up her small children. All the while, she successfully climbed the immensely male-dominated ladder of trade-union politics. That she succeeded so magnificently is an enormous tribute to her and a heart-warming story for the rest of us. This is a great book for anyone who thinks life has dealt them an impossible hand. Margaret shows how the impossible became possible.

Against this backdrop, with the odds stacked against her, Margaret's story is also that of a political and social trailblazer. I remember, early in my career, how unwelcoming some parts of the Labour movement were to women. Since then, progress on that front has been good and we're a world away from the 1970s and 1980s. But that change didn't happen overnight and it was far from inevitable. It happened because Margaret and others fought against the status quo and refused to accept attitudes that too many in the Labour movement felt were acceptable. And she got important issues such as equal pay on to the agenda in the process.

Long before her political journey made Margaret into the activist I know now, she worked with some of the most deprived people in our society as an adviser in a South

London law centre, helping those caught in the tentacles of circumstance. Those experiences at work, as well as others closer to home, clearly had an impact on Margaret, reinforcing her determination to strive for those in need for the many years that followed.

Her career in the Transport and General Workers' Union, culminating in her role as deputy general secretary and then president of the Trade Union Congress, saw Margaret push for equality, day in, day out, for twenty years. This really is the story of a great woman who successfully drove change in what was essentially a man's world, convincing others to adapt to the modern world around them.

Her determination and experience made her perfect for the roles she would later take up as we in the Labour Party got into a position where we could do more than just talk. Those were heady times, but the challenges we faced after so long in opposition were immense and many, like Margaret, rose to that challenge.

The social progress made in the 1990s and 2000s, when government started to catch up with the changing world, was possible because people such as Margaret started to apply their years of experience. Her work was invaluable in her roles as chair of the Women and Work Commission, as a member of the Low Pay Commission—which has helped the minimum wage we introduced keep up with the times—and at the Equality and Human Rights Commission. Quite simply, Britain is a more equal place because of people such as Margaret. The Britain that countries around the world look to for inspiration in developing their own democracies is inspiring because Margaret and others never stopped striving for other people. They never stopped applying their values of fairness and equal opportunities for all in every role they took on.

I came across Margaret when she was already quite senior in the T&G. I then worked closely with her over more than a decade. Throughout that time, what impressed me most was her integrity. She was canny—she had to be in that type of politics. She was politically very astute. But she never compromised her essential principles or decency. She never let me down, even when it was hard for her to carry on supporting me, and she showed enormous courage when she came under attack. She was a big part of getting the Labour Party into power and a big part in keeping it there. She was especially passionate, for obvious reasons, about the rights of women, but always in a way that was designed to win maximum support, not to alienate people.

She believed in the trade union movement, but she also knew it had to change with the times and, in particular, she was deeply impatient with the so-called traditions of the movement that were really just another way of protecting its vested, and especially masculine, interests! Margaret is a great leader, a great woman and a great fighter for human rights everywhere. This is someone whose life is worth studying.

Tony Blair

Prologue

EVEN AFTER ALL THESE YEARS, I can still remember sitting at the table in the scullery one morning when I was ten, watching my mum making the pastry for an apple pie. She turned to me suddenly, dusting the flour from her hands, and said solemnly, 'Margie, you should live within your station in life.'

I think I was probably showing off at the time. I nodded, even though I didn't really understand what she meant: 'Yes, Mum.'

'Always remember that,' she said.

And I have. But I've also realized that my mum was wrong. I didn't discover this, though, until many years later. I grew up believing that it was important to know your place in the world and that you had to fit in and not make a fuss. Like many working-class women of her generation, my mum didn't think that it was possible to move out of your social group. I can understand this, as women like her had very few opportunities back then. But the truth is that we don't have to conform to the way others might expect us to live. If we expand our horizons, work hard and aim high, we can achieve so much.

Maybe, though, somewhere at the back of her mind, Mum sensed this, because she would also say to me, 'You're no better than anyone else; but you're no worse either.' She was dead right about this. Although I grew up in a working-class family, I had the unusual experience of going to a posh school. Yet I never once felt in any way inferior to the other pupils just because they lived in big houses and had wealthy parents. Believing that I am no better or worse than anyone else has been one of my guiding principles throughout my life.

And my life has had its fair share of ups and downs. While I grew up in a family that was very loving, my parents had low expectations of me. I left school with no qualifications and got a job in an office. When I became pregnant at the age of twenty, I did what most girls did in the 1950s and got married. But the marriage quickly turned sour. Then my husband became paralysed and ended up in a wheelchair, and I found myself struggling to care for him around the clock while bringing up our three children on social security benefits. At the time we were living on the sixteenth floor of a tower block on a council estate in South London.

It wasn't until I was in my late thirties, when I took up community advice work in Southwark, that I started to discover my hidden potential and grow in confidence. I'm living proof that you can do badly at school and still go on to achieve things later in life. I didn't gain my first qualification—an O level—until I was nearly forty.

When I landed a job with the Transport and General Workers' Union (T&G), I found myself in a man's world. The fact that on the floor in Transport House where the executive committee met there was no ladies' loo said it all. Women were seen as second-class citizens in the T&G in those days, and anything concerning them wasn't seen as an industrial issue.

I was determined to be judged on how well I did my job, not on being a woman—but, of course, there were those who refused to accept me on these terms. Charlotte Whitton, the first woman to become mayor of Ottawa, said, 'Whatever a woman does she must do it twice as well as a man to be thought half as good,' and then added, 'Luckily this is not difficult.' She was spot on. Given some of the attitudes I encountered in senior figures, I might easily have quit the union and taken another kind of job, where I wouldn't have had so many battles.

But I've never been a quitter. So I stayed for nineteen years, fighting hard to get issues that particularly affected and concerned women on the agenda. The film *Made in*

Dagenham, which told the story of a group of women at the Ford car factory who went on strike, captured something of the way working women were treated. I found other like-minded women in the trade-union movement and we worked hard to change attitudes and policies.

Despite the obstacles I encountered at the T&G, I went on to become deputy general secretary, the first woman to hold this post. It's an achievement of which I'm very proud. Something else I'm proud of is serving as TUC president for a year.

My career in the trade-union movement provided me with opportunities to travel to countries such as Russia, South Africa, Palestine and Fiji, where I met women struggling for equal rights and learnt about how unions were trying to improve the pay and conditions of workers. I also nearly got tear-gassed when I took part in a demonstration in Chile.

Alongside my union work, I was an active member of the Labour Party, and I became its treasurer just before Tony Blair led it to victory in the 1997 general election. Most people today seem to have a low opinion of politicians and, to a certain extent, I can understand why. But during my time on the Labour Party national executive committee, when Tony Blair was trying to change the face of British politics, I saw at first hand the complexities surrounding political decisions and also the human failings of those we elect. Yet I believe the vast majority of MPs are committed to trying to make a difference. Whether or not you believe in what they say, most of the time *they* actually believe it. And almost every one of them works extremely hard.

After retiring from the T&G I found exciting new opportunities and challenges. By far the most unexpected was serving on the board of Royal Mail. For the first time, I found myself sitting on the other side of the industrial fence.

When I was growing up I always thought people with fancy titles came from posh families, not families from council estates. But in 2004 I entered the House of Lords, which meant I became a Baroness, or Lady. But it's not the title that really matters to me; it's the chance to try to influence and shape the legislation passing through parliament.

It's thanks to legislation such as the Sex Discrimination Act that women are now entitled to be treated as equal to men at work—and everywhere else. While a lot of progress has been made in giving women the same opportunities as men, much more still needs to be done when it comes to things such as affordable childcare, pay and training opportunities. And much more still needs to be done to bring about a fairer society not just for women, but for men as well.

The reason I've written my story is not only to attempt to make some sense out of my life and pull some of the threads together—something most of us feel the urge to do as we get older—but also to inspire others, especially women, to go out and try to make a difference in the world. If you believe that you can do this, then you can go on to achieve things you have never dreamt of. That's exactly what happened to me.

1. A Double Life

MY STORY BEGINS on 22 August 1937 in Gladstone Terrace, a six-storey tenement building in Battersea, a working-class area of south-west London. It's hard to imagine now that in those days it was normal for several families to share a sink on the landing. When I was seven months old, my parents moved a couple of miles away to a small two-bedroomed terraced house in Coteford Street, in Tooting. In fact, the houses were known as cottages and were part of the Totterdown Estate, built by the London County Council. We had a living room and scullery downstairs, with a coal cellar underneath the stairs. My mum and dad had one bedroom and I shared the other with my three sisters—Vera, who was eight years older, Pam, who was six years older and Marion, who was two years older. We didn't have a bathroom or inside toilet. Instead we had to use a tin bath and go to the loo in a shed at the end of the back garden. I remember the house being very brown.

Mum and Dad came from South London. She was a Barry and was born in Fulham to Irish parents, who were heavy drinkers and, from what I can make out, incapable of raising a family. This was why, when she was five, she and her sisters and brothers ended up living in children's homes, including one near Salisbury in Wiltshire run by nuns. It was a very harsh and regimented place, where the children were not encouraged to use their imaginations. She had to get up early each morning and then rummage in a box for a pair of boots that fitted her. I remember her telling me how cold the nuns were and that sometimes they used to hit her on her knuckles with a broom handle. They hit her so hard that they broke her fingers. When she was sixteen she left the children's home and returned to live with her parents in Fulham.

Many years later, my mum was on holiday with one of my sisters, and they drove to the gates of the children's home.

Seeing the home again, all those painful memories came flooding back and she burst into tears.

When I think about it now, I find it amazing that, despite this experience at the hands of the nuns, she was able to bring us up in a loving and caring way, because she must have been badly damaged by what she went through. I think this was because she wanted us to have what she had never had. Mind you, she did give me a really good walloping one time when I was fourteen. I'd been out with my friends wandering around the shops in Streatham High Road and, when I came back, she asked me to put the kettle on. I decided I didn't want to and told her to do it. She leapt out of her chair and grabbed hold of me and whacked me on the backside. I didn't backchat her again.

Dad was one of six children and grew up in Battersea. He was a James. His parents were better off than my mum's. His father had owned a greengrocer's shop at one time. When I was born, Dad was working in a factory in Clapham. After the war, he found work on building sites. While my mum always dressed plainly, my dad seemed quite dashing. He had thick black hair, which reminded me of patent leather. He would stand looking in the mirror in the kitchen, carefully smoothing his hair down with a knob of dripping.

My dad lived by clear moral principles and he had strong views on how you should behave. For example, he didn't approve of vulgar language and he didn't like it if someone started talking about a woman who might have had too much to drink. He was always very considerate towards others. When he travelled on the Tube, he always wore clean trousers and shoes, not his building-site clothes, because he didn't want to make the seats dirty.

His main interests were doing puzzles and crosswords, and playing cards. He would sit at the table in the living room in the evenings playing whist on his own, every now and again lighting up a Woodbine. He was very easy-going and tolerant and always deferred to my mum if there was a problem. She made most of the decisions in the family, but I think she used to get a bit browned off with this. She didn't express a lot of emotion, but she wasn't a miserable or angry person. If she disagreed with my dad about anything, she would just raise her eyebrows.

Although both Mum and Dad were very intelligent, they weren't qualified to do anything other than unskilled work. My mum did a variety of jobs when I was growing up. She cleaned people's houses and worked part-time at Pascall's sweet factory and at a toy factory, which were both in Mitcham. Her way of relaxing was to read. She loved travel books and fiction.

Politics didn't play much of a part in life at home. The only time it was ever spoken of was during a general election. My mum always voted Conservative and read the *Daily Express*, while my dad voted Labour and read the *Daily Mirror*. I don't think my mum thought much of politicians. Like a lot of people, she believed they were just out for their own ends.

I remember the years of the Second World War as an exciting time. We used to lay sheets of corrugated iron over the huge craters that the bombs had made and then run over them. We also used to make grottos from pieces of broken china, glass, stones and flowers and sit on Franciscan Road, which ran down from Tooting Bec Common, and ask the commuters walking down from the bus stop for a ha'penny. Some days we made quite a bit of money. People must have thought we were proper little urchins.

At the bottom of our back garden was an Anderson shelter with bunks in it. It was gloomy and cold and stank of dampness. Even now, I can still hear the wail of the air-raid siren. I was never afraid when I heard it, because I was too young to really understand what was happening. When we sat in the half-light of the shelter, I could sense from the anxious expressions on the faces of Mum and Dad that something wasn't quite right.

My dad had attached a rope to the back door so we could swing on it and land on top of the shelter. It was great fun. Once when the siren sounded, I was in the street, playing with my friends. And I just ignored it. I remember I was wearing a green tweed coat my mum had bought for me in Marks and Spencer. I looked up to see her running down the street towards me, her arms outstretched, and looking very angry.

Life was austere during the war. Like everyone else, we received rations and enjoyed few luxuries. My mum could make a shilling last like a pound. She was very organized and thrifty. Marion and I would often take the potato and carrot peelings to a woman down the road who kept chickens and she would give us eggs for them. Mum used to give one of our neighbours used tea-leaves and she would give us lovely juicy black cherries from a tree in her garden. I can remember often being sent to a grocer's to see if he had any oranges for sale, or to Tooting market to buy eggs.

I can also remember going to Smith's department store on Tooting Broadway to try and buy combs. We all had really thick hair and I used to have to tie the plaits in my hair with a belt from an old dress. One day my mum sighed and said to me, 'You can't buy anything nice, not even a comb or some nice hair ribbon.' She must have been really fed up.

All our clothes were serviceable. We wore warm skirts, double-breasted coats. I used to wear my sisters' clothes when they no longer fitted them. I remember a green and yellow Fair Isle jumper that had shrunk because it had been washed so many times.

We would sometimes sit in front of the range in the living room and make rag rugs. We did this by cutting up old coats into little strips of cloth and, using a hook, pulling them through a piece of sacking which was backed by another material. We put the rugs in front of the doors to keep the draught out.

We usually had just bread and milk for breakfast. I found it disgusting and, once my mum had gone out, I'd go into the back garden and tip it over the fence. Instead I'd get some dripping from the bowl in the cupboard. My mum made the dripping by cutting off the fat from a joint of meat and melting it in the oven. The smell was horrible. I'd wrap the dripping in paper, and, on my way to school, buy a hot bread roll from the baker's in Franciscan Road and spread the dripping on it. One of my favourite meals was bacon roly-poly, which was suet pastry rolled up with bacon in the middle, like a Swiss roll. It was delicious. Because of rationing, we didn't get sweets very often. Instead we bought Ovaltine tablets in a tin.

I always had plenty to say for myself. I was never backward in coming forward. In fact, my mum used to pay me a penny to shut up for an hour. One day, I asked her why she didn't wear a wedding ring. All the other mums I knew wore one, and I was puzzled about why my mum didn't. She avoided the question. Later, I discovered from one of my sisters that she had pawned it because she had been short of money.

To celebrate the end of the war in 1945, we had a street party. Bunting hung across the street and Union Jacks were draped from upstairs windows. We all sat at long trestle tables, piled with sandwiches, bottles of orange juice, jelly and cakes. Someone played an accordion and a neighbour did acrobatics. In the evening, people lit bonfires in the street.

Although my mum was married in a Catholic church and she brought us all up as Catholics, because of the treatment she had received from the nuns in the children's home, she didn't have very warm feelings towards the Church.

Sometimes a priest from the parish would call and ask her why she didn't go to Mass. She would always reply, 'I've spent enough years of my life on my knees, thank you, Father.'

I went to St Boniface's Catholic primary school in Undine Street, Tooting. It was very strict. If you misbehaved, Mrs Hinsby, my class teacher, would come up behind you and smack your legs.

I remember my childhood as a time of great freedom. I had lots of friends in Tooting, and they were always knocking at the door for me. We used to play skipping and knock down ginger in the street. In the school holidays we often went to Tooting Bec Common, where we'd climb trees and spend hours just running around and then sit on the grass and eat our sandwiches. On the way there, we often bought lemonade or raspberryade from a shop run by a man everyone called 'Uncle'. He was a fat bloke with wispy grey hair and he always wore overalls. He made the drinks himself. We would peer through the iron railings of the mental hospital, which backed on to the common, hoping to see some of the patients. Afterwards, we'd walk to St Leonard's church in Streatham to look at the headstones in the graveyard. The inscriptions fascinated me.

Sunday lunch was the high point of the week. We all sat around the table for a traditional dinner of roast lamb or beef, potatoes and vegetables. My mum kept the meat in a meat safe, a wooden board covered by muslin, to keep the flies away. I don't know why, but I always got the giggles when we were all sitting around the table, and then my sisters would start giggling My dad would smile and say, 'You daft buggers. You'd laugh to see a pudding run.' That made us giggle even more.

I used to go to the Granada cinema in Tooting with mum. But most of the films we watched were ones that she wanted to see. I can still remember watching *Henry V*, starring

Laurence Olivier, and not understanding a word of it. What I remember most is sitting there waiting for the film to begin and then seeing the cinema organ rising up with a man sitting at it.

A big treat was to catch the Tube to the West End and go to the Palladium for a show and then afterwards get something to eat in a Lyons Corner House in Coventry Street, just off Leicester Square. I remember the gold-edged mirrors and how white the tablecloths and linen napkins were. At Christmas we'd often go to a pantomime in the West End or at the theatre in Streatham Hill.

We usually visited Auntie Dolly, one of my mum's sisters, the week before Christmas. She lived in a spacious flat at the top of a house in Battersea and seemed posh, because she had a piano in the living room. She worked as an area manageress for Lyons tea shops. Uncle Harold was a grocer at Home and Colonial, a chain of stores.

In the summer we went for days out to Ramsgate, Margate, Hastings and other resorts on the south coast. I can still recall the excitement I felt when, carrying our sandwiches and flasks and buckets and spades, we'd climb aboard either a Grey Green or Orange coach in Balham early in the morning. We had a wonderful time, paddling in the sea, making sandcastles and going on the rides in the amusement parks. On the journey back, the coach would stop somewhere so that we could pick bluebells and buy cherries from the people who sold them at the roadside.

I wasn't very daring as a child and I didn't have any great ambition to do or be anything. My parents expected that when I left school I'd just get a decent office job.

My sisters couldn't have been more different. Vera, the eldest, was quite idle and had very little patience with me. She was supposed to look after us on the rare occasions when Mum and Dad went out together. But instead she would go off and meet her friends and leave us indoors on our own. I can remember Marion and me standing on the corner of the road in our nightdresses waiting for Mum and Dad to come round the corner.

Vera left home when she was sixteen, joined the Women's Land Army and was sent to somewhere near Ipswich. When she returned, she was tanned and she'd dyed her hair blonde. But she also gave us all head lice and scabies. She eventually got an office job with the Conservative Party in Smith Square.

Pam was a home bird and loved cooking. When she was eight she learnt how to knit jumpers. She was given a scholarship to the Oratory School in South Kensington. Marion was the quietest of us all and very timid. We often argued over the radio. Pam would want to listen to a music programme and Marion and I would want to listen to Larry the Lamb on *Children's Hour*.

When I was eight my sisters and I and my dad all caught scarlet fever. I had a rash all over my skin. The doctor was in and out of the house all the time. At one point, I was so ill that my mum and dad thought I was going to die. But something good came out of this. The doctor informed the council that we were living in overcrowded conditions and, as a result, the LCC decided to move us to a new house in Carshalton, a much more leafy area. We were all excited because we would have a bathroom and hot running water for the first time. Although I knew I'd miss my friends in Tooting, I didn't feel anxious, as I always found it easy to make new friends.

The house was on Wrythe Lane on the St Helier Estate, built in the 1930s to rehouse families from inner London. It contained around nine thousand houses and flats, along with several pubs, churches and a cinema. Our house had two bedrooms upstairs and a downstairs room divided by double doors into a lounge and bedroom. It had a back and front garden. In front of it was a large green.

Not long after we moved, we went back to the house in Tooting, probably to get something we'd forgotten. When some of the neighbours saw us walking down the street, they called out, 'Oh, gone to the country, have you, and left us behind?'

Mum and Dad spent most of their time at home. The only time Dad went out was after tea on Saturday evenings when he'd put on his suit and say, 'I'm just going for a mooch.' He'd catch a bus to Morden and then take the Northern Line to the West End, where he'd spend a couple of hours wandering around the streets before going for a drink in a pub. He never drank much. He was quite happy just sipping a couple of halves of bitter.

I attended St Mary's primary school in Carshalton for a short while, where I sat the common entrance exam. In those days everyone did. I was offered a scholarship at either St Philomena's, which was next to St Mary's, or the Ursuline Convent in Wimbledon, both private schools. Because it was just a short bus ride away, my parents chose St Philomena's school, which was run by the Daughters of the Cross.

St Philomena's was an imposing three-storey, eighteenth-century red-brick building that had once been Carshalton House, the home of a tobacco merchant. It was situated at the end of a long drive and set in beautiful parkland, surrounded by high walls. The grounds contained an indoor swimming pool, tennis courts, a lacrosse field and a lake with a stone bridge across it.

My mum took me for an interview with Sister Mary Winifred, the mother superior. I can remember walking through the main entrance and then climbing a sweeping teak staircase and walking down an oak-panelled corridor that led to her office. Sister Mary Winifred was sitting behind a huge desk. She was wearing a black and white religious habit with a large cross around her neck and looked very serious and a little scary. I found myself staring at her, as she asked Mum about my education and what I wanted to do after I left school. I can't remember what my mum said, but I can remember Sister Mary Winifred saying in a patronizing voice, 'Very well, we'll take her.'

She told my mum that she had to buy my school uniform from a shop in Kensington High Street called Daniel Neale. My mum nearly fainted, as she knew that this meant it would be very expensive.

When we came out of the interview, Mum was stony-faced.

'What's the matter, Mum?' I asked.

'Did you see the way she looked us up and down?'

'What do you mean?'

'She doesn't think we are good enough. Margie?'

'What, Mum?'

'Always remember that you're no better than anyone else; but you're no worse either.'

Somehow Mum found the money for my uniform. We wore a brown tunic, cream blouse and brown coat and hat. Our tie was blue, cream and orange. In the summer we wore blue gingham checked dresses and straw panama hats.

The school only admitted two common entrance exam pupils each year. The other girls at St Philomena's came from well-to-do families. Many of them were boarders. There were two streams. As a scholarship girl I was put in the top stream. I studied science, Latin, English literature, RE, maths and needlework. We were divided into houses, named after saints. I was in St George's. I can remember the smell of floor polish in the long corridors and the nuns scattering dried tea leaves over the floor to help them sweep up the dust.

Most of the teachers were nuns and many of them seemed to be upper-class. They were all English. Sister Mary Joanna, my form tutor, was young and pretty. Sister Mary Rosa taught needlework (once a pupil stuck a pin in her: the girl was suspended but, because her father was a US diplomat, she was allowed to return). When Sister Mary Bernadette, the headmistress, was sent to work in Africa, we all thought this was sad, as she would suffer from the heat because she was very fat.

As it was a Catholic school, we were taught a lot of RE, and each lesson began with a prayer and the sign of the cross. We also had to attend services in the chapel, which was beautifully decorated and had high stained-glass windows.

The Catholicism of the nuns shaped my knowledge of the wider world. I became aware of Communism, because the nuns told us how religion was banned in Communist countries and how Catholics were persecuted. We were told about a cardinal who was in prison somewhere. We all had to pray for the conversion of Russia. We also learnt about African babies and were urged to collect money in envelopes for them.

Every term, we had a deportment competition. The teachers used to observe our behaviour as we went around the school. I won it when I was thirteen. My name was read out at the morning assembly and I had to go up on to the stage to receive a red sash, which I wore in place of my tunic belt. Everyone applauded when I stepped off the stage and returned to my seat. I felt very proud. When I told Mum and Dad that evening they were thrilled.

I soon became aware that the other pupils came from a different world from me. They lived in big houses and their parents were very well-to-do. Most of their parents owned cars, which was not common back then. One girl's father was a manager at the Bank of Australia and another's owned a factory that canned fruit and vegetables. I remember one girl arriving every morning in a huge silver and green Austin Princess, driven by her mum. A German girl came to school one day with a Slazenger tennis racket, which cost five pounds. I was amazed, as this was what my dad earned in a week. I remember her telling me with great excitement how she had learnt to peel a potato. There was also a girl from Florida. Even though she was from such a sunny place, she was very pale. She ate her meals with just a fork, which I thought was very strange.

The school organized tennis tournaments for parents. My mum and dad never took part, as they had never been given the opportunity to learn how to play it. But I didn't mind, as they would have only embarrassed me.

But the other girls didn't look down on me because I lived on a council estate. I was never made to feel that I wasn't as good as they were. When one of my friends gave me a present and I showed it to my dad, he said to my mum, 'She must be very popular.' She just tutted, as she didn't approve of him praising me. I think she thought I had too high an opinion of myself anyway.

Sometimes I used to go with a friend to her large house in Purley. In the summer holidays, she would often invite me to go with her to her aunt's and uncle's farm near Tenterden in Kent. I really enjoyed this taste of the country. Her aunt and uncle were very kind and used to take us for tea to the Copper Kettle café. But I also felt homesick and always looked forward to going home.

My favourite subject was English. I had always enjoyed reading, particularly Enid Blyton and A. J. Cronin novels. When I was eleven, I came top of my year in spelling. But I didn't work that hard because, unlike the other girls, I wasn't ambitious to get on in life. It felt like I was leading a double life at school. In the day I was mixing with girls from wealthy backgrounds; and then when I went home to the council estate I was mixing with girls from quite poor families. Although I enjoyed visiting my friends at their homes and seeing how they lived, I never felt envious or wanted the kind of lifestyle they had. My friends on the estate didn't mind that I went to a posh school, but some of the other kids used to call me names when I walked past them in the street. The fact that I was wearing a brown velvet hat didn't help.

Mixing with girls from different backgrounds helped me to realize that just because you had a lot of money it didn't mean that you were any different from anyone else. I also realized that the pupils at St Philomena's weren't any brighter than my friends on the council estate, and the only reason these girls got into St Philomena's was because their parents had money. It wasn't because they were academically outstanding. While St Philomena's had so many fantastic facilities, St Mary's, on the other hand, had nothing. This taught me one of my most important early lessons: that life wasn't fair.

When I was fourteen I went away on holiday for the first time. We went for a week to a holiday camp at Dymchurch in Kent. What I remember most about it is that it was very damp.

I must have been about twelve when I joined the Girl Guides in Hackbridge, becoming a leader in the Daffodil Patrol. We went camping on farms in Midhurst and Cuckfield in Sussex, travelling there in the back of a bumpy lorry. I remember that we would be sent off to gather twigs and then make things such as tripods and toothbrush racks with them. We were sent into the woods to identify different kinds of trees and flowers, and then we'd have to draw them and write about them. The highlight was in the late afternoon when we would all sit around the camp fire and sing songs. I loved it.

When I became a tent leader, I learnt that being a leader was not about power and glory. I had to get up in the middle of the night and close the flaps of the tents if it rained. I would end up soaked and covered in mud. Two of the most important lessons being a Guide taught me were how to use your time constructively and how to rub along in difficult circumstances. These have stood me in good stead throughout my life.

I decided I wanted to leave school when I was fifteen. I didn't want to continue studying as all the other girls were planning to do. I just wanted to get a job and become a grown-up, like my sisters. Over lunch in the dining room one day, a friend asked me what I was going to do after leaving school. She said she was planning to go to university.

'I don't know,' I replied.

She looked shocked. 'You don't know?'

I shook my head. 'My mum and dad don't want me to stay on.' It wasn't strictly true. When I told my mum and dad that I wanted to leave, they just accepted my decision. They would have probably done the same had I said I was staying on.

'They don't?'

'And anyway my friends at the secondary modern are leaving when they are fifteen.'

However, unlike my parents, the nuns had high expectations. When I went to see Sister Mary Winifred in her office one morning and told her that I wanted to leave she looked very cross.

'Well, it looks like giving you the scholarship was a waste,' she sighed.

When she said this, I was overcome by guilt. Had I wasted it? Would it have been better if someone else had been given the scholarship? But in my mind I didn't equate going to St Philomena's with examinations and a place at university. I just thought of it as going to a good school. And that's how my mum and dad saw it. Sister Mary Winifred tried to persuade me to continue with my studies. But I was adamant that I was going to leave, even though I didn't have a clue what kind of job I wanted.

2. Wedding Bells

AFTER I LEFT SCHOOL in the summer of 1953 my mum decided to write to companies advertising in the *Evening Standard* for juniors in their accounts departments. She thought it was respectable sort of work for a girl. I wasn't particularly good with figures, but Mum told me that you didn't need to be to work in accounts. 'You just have to work hard and do your best.'

One morning, she received a letter from Marshall and Snelgrove, a large department store in Oxford Street, inviting me to an interview. I was thrilled, but also anxious, as I'd never been for a job interview before. I was pleased when my mum said that she would come with me. I knew it was important to make a good impression, so I put on my best white cotton dress with a blue cardigan.

'What will they ask me?' I said to Mum, as we made our way along Oxford Street.

'Just about your education and why you want the job. There's nothing to worry about.'

But I was worried. What if I said the wrong thing? And what if I was asked about accounts? I knew nothing at all about this.

At the store, we were directed to the personnel office, where we were told to take a seat in a reception area. Sitting there, looking at people in suits coming and going, I felt very self-conscious.

Eventually we were called into an office with lots of files on shelves, where a smartly dressed woman was sitting behind a desk. She stood up, smiled and shook my hand.

'So, Margaret, you would like to work for us, would you?'

'Yes,' I said.

'Very good. Tell me about why you would like to work in accounts.'

I struggled for something to say, eventually blurting out, 'I think I would be good at it.'

'I see. And what were you like at school?'

'My attendance record was very good and I was never late.'

'Excellent. Attendance and punctuality are two of the most important things in a job.'

I nodded. 'Yes.'

She asked me a few more questions, but I can't remember what I replied. At the end of the interview, she said, 'Very well, we'll take you on. You'll start next Monday at nine o'clock.'

'Thank you,' I said, hardly able to believe that I now had a job.

Mum was delighted, and told me that I had found a very good job. I felt over the moon and couldn't wait to get back to Carshalton to tell my friends. I didn't mind the long journey each day, because I felt that working in the West End was far more interesting than working near home. It would sound glamorous when I told people I worked in Oxford Street.

The following Monday morning I left home at 7.30 a.m. and caught the bus to Morden, where I took the Tube. I arrived at the side door to the store and was told to go through a scruffy basement containing lockers for the staff and take the staff lift to the top floor. The supervisor met me and showed into a large office where a dozen or so women, all older than me, were sitting at desks laid out around the edge of the room. In the middle were ten National 3000 accounting machines, each with a chair in front of it. She told me to sit at a desk by the window, explaining that my job was to go through piles of sales receipts from account holders and enter the figures against their names in the ledger. Once this was done, the information needed to be written on an invoice, which would be sent to the customer.

The office was very regimented. If I wanted to go to the toilet, I had to ask permission from the supervisor. She would say, 'Be quick. Come straight back.' One day, it was discovered that two of the women hadn't logged their invoices but had taken them home to the hostel in the East End where they lived. We were all called into a room and informed by one of the managers that the girls had stolen from the company and wouldn't be coming back. This all seemed shocking.

At lunchtime, I'd sometimes meet some friends who were working in offices nearby and we'd go to a small, dark basement jazz club in Greek Street in Soho to hang out and dance and listen to music. There would always be quite a few West Indian men there, most of them having only recently arrived in London. I can still remember hearing Bill Haley's 'Rock Around the Clock' for the first time. As I only had an hour for lunch, I had to run there and back. No wonder I was so skinny.

Once I had learnt how to operate the accounting machine, I quickly got bored. I found the work monotonous, and soon after I registered with an employment agency and began looking for another job.

I was offered a job in the accounts department at the offices of ABC Cinemas in Soho. One of its attractions was that I wouldn't have to work every second Saturday, as I had done at Marshall and Snelgrove.

Working for a cinema company might have seemed glamorous, but it wasn't. My job involved taking the monthly figures for the sale of tickets, confectionery and drinks at cinemas, keying them into an accounting machine and then attaching the receipts to a beige card.

The atmosphere wasn't as strict as at Marshall and Snelgrove. We'd work our socks off for two weeks and then have little to do for the next fortnight. So we'd sit around, chatting and reading magazines until we got busy again.

When Pam, who was working for a building company in Beddington, got married in 1954, I was one of her bridesmaids. She and her husband then came to live with us. This made the house seem very crowded and caused arguments between us. We had always got on well, but now I felt resentful and thought they should find their own place to live. I was a stupid teenager. But back then there wasn't much rented property available. I was relieved when, after a year or so, they moved to Stevenage in Hertfordshire.

I loved listening to music. When we bought a radiogram, I used to sit in the front room listening to jazz, especially Sarah Vaughan and Ella Fitzgerald, my favourite singers. At weekends I often went dancing. My favourite places were the Streatham Locarno, the Hammersmith Palais and the Wimbledon Palais. On occasions, I'd go to the Lyceum in the West End. Before we went there, we'd go to the Black and White Milk Bar in Leicester Square. Unlike in the jazz club I used to go to, all the white men at the Lyceum would stand on one side of the dance floor and all the black men on the other side. There was very little mixing between them. On Sundays, my friends and I would often meet in a café on the estate and then, later, go to the London Palladium to see the Ted Heath Band or another top dance band. It only cost half a crown to get in.

When I went out with my friends I began to meet boys, of course. I had a good choice of boyfriends. I always seemed to end up with ones who were good-looking. I wasn't really interested in going out with any of the boys on the estate. I preferred the ones I'd see in the West End, as they seemed more exciting. I wasn't looking to find a regular boyfriend and get married, but I knew that, eventually, this is what would happen.

Sometimes my friend Doreen and I would go to a pub on the St Helier Estate and—after nipping into the ladies' to make sure we looked all right—buy half a shandy between us and sit in the corner, hoping some of the boys would buy us a drink. This always worked.

Doreen got married, but soon after had an affair with a married man called Charlie. He was part of a group whom we guessed to be involved in crime of one sort or another. One of his friends was called Buster. One afternoon, her husband returned home unexpectedly and her lover had to leap out of the back window.

After a couple of years at ABC I got a job in the accounts office with Holland, Hannen and Cubitts, a construction company in Queen Anne's Gate, near St James' Park underground station. I worked in a basement with four other women and a supervisor. I was now earning more money than my dad, who still worked on building sites. He wasn't paid that well, so he used to buy a workman's ticket for the Tube but charge his company for a full one.

In the summer of 1957 Doreen and I went to a Butlin's holiday camp in Skegness, and one evening I met a handsome man called Joe, who had just left the army. We had a drink in the bar with him and his mates. He seemed very charming and funny. He told me he came from Edgware and worked for his dad, who was a coal merchant. When I asked him why he was so tanned, he said he'd been stationed in Tripoli in Libya.

I liked him and, when I returned to Carshalton, we met again and soon started going out with each other. We weren't able to see each other that often, as it was a long journey from North London to Carshalton. I eventually invited him round to meet my parents, and they seemed to like him. Around Christmas time he proposed to me and I accepted. It was what you would call a whirlwind romance.

Soon after, I became worried that I might be pregnant, so I made an appointment to see my GP. I found it very hard having to discuss my private life with him. He concluded that my fears were right. I was pregnant.

I came away from the surgery with my head swirling. I'd never really thought that much about getting pregnant. As the news sank in, I felt frightened and anxious. I'd felt so in control of my life, but now I was going to have to be a mother. I didn't feel I was ready for it.

When I met Joe a few days later, I said, 'Joe, there's something I have to tell you.'

'What?'

'I'm pregnant.'

'You're pregnant!'

I nodded. 'My doctor told me.'

'That's great!'

I felt relived that Joe was pleased. I hadn't known how he might react.

I dreaded having to tell my mum. I felt I had let her down and that she would feel hurt. One morning, I sat down at the table with her. 'Mum, I've something to tell you,' I said.

'What is it?' she replied, looking serious.

'I'm pregnant.'

She looked at me for a moment and then said, 'I knew there was something wrong, Margie. You've not been your normal cheery self.'

I could tell she was sad, not because she was ashamed of me but because she could see that I was going to find it difficult adapting to marriage and a baby at the same time.

When I told my dad later that evening when he came back from work, he nodded silently in his armchair, took a sip of tea, and said, 'Well, that's a shame. I'm sorry about it. So, we have to think what we are going to do.'

Joe and I got married at Holy Cross Catholic church in Carshalton on a bright, cold day on 15 February 1958. We had a reception at home. It wasn't a flash affair, as neither of us had much money. I remember we had pork pie, pickles, beetroot and salad.

After the reception, Joe's dad drove us across London to Cricklewood, where we had rented a room. I wasn't keen on him. He was a burly man who was vulgar and bad-tempered, and he got worse the more he drank. I was sitting in the back of the car with Joe, his mum and his brother George. Joe's granny was sitting in the front. As we drove up Edgware Road, Joe's dad began arguing with George over something. The next minute, he pulled the car over to the side of the road and ordered him to get out. I sat there, feeling scared.

A few weeks later, Joe's granny died and we inherited her tenancy in a grotty Victorian house in Medley Road, Kilburn. We lived on the middle floor and had our own living room, kitchen and bedroom, but we had to share the bathroom and toilet (which didn't flush properly) with Mrs Smith and her boyfriend, an Irish builder, who lived above us. There was no running hot water in the house and it was full of mice. I'd see them scurrying across the kitchen floor and disappearing through gaps in the floorboards or skirting boards. I hated the place.

Below us lived Mr and Mrs Vaughan. She was Welsh and he drove a Schweppes lorry. They had a little girl and a son who was a teenager.

Even though I made friends with several families in my street, I didn't like living in Kilburn. With its neat houses and sense of community, Carshalton was quite a settled place. Kilburn, on the other hand, was much more transient. Most of its houses had been divided into rooms, many of which were occupied by newly arrived West Indian families or Irish labourers working on building sites or digging the roads. I used to see groups of men standing on street corners in the morning, waiting to be picked up by a van and taken to a building site somewhere. After they finished work, they would crowd into the pubs and spend the evenings drinking. I can remember once walking down Kilburn High Road and seeing a group of them fighting on the back of a lorry. The Irish population was so large that they built an extension to St Anne's Catholic church in Quex Road. I remember an Irish friend who was having an affair telling me she would go to Mass and receive communion and then take the pill afterwards. She said she felt it was wrong to take it before.

I found married life difficult. I didn't know what I was supposed to do. I didn't know how to cook or look after a home. The romance that had sparked the relationship with Joe quickly evaporated.

Whereas my dad would peel potatoes or carry heavy shopping, when Joe came home from work, his face covered in coal dust, he would have a wash in the sink and then just sit in the chair, looking morose. He would spent most evenings watching the TV we rented. As he had to get up very early for the coal round with his dad, we went to bed early. In the summer when we went to bed it was still daylight. Because there wasn't work in the summer, he found a job in a local factory and then became a bus driver. He was based at the garage in Cricklewood and would often drive the number 16.

I think he began to feel trapped. It wasn't long before tensions started to emerge between us and we began arguing a lot. Once, I was sitting at the table flicking through a newspaper while he was watching one of his favourite programmes and he got really annoyed with me. He didn't like the idea that I was doing something on my own. I was often on edge when he came back from work. I never knew whether he'd be in a good mood or whether he'd be grumpy. As the months went by, I found myself becoming really unhappy. I'd always been very chatty, but with Joe I found myself saying very little and becoming withdrawn. I worried what life would be like when our child was born.

During my pregnancy I felt drained for much of the time and was constantly throwing up. Even doing simple things, such as cooking and washing, took a real effort. I lay awake at night worrying about how I would cope once I had given birth. What made me even more worried was that the hospital had told me I would have to have the baby at home. I wanted to be in hospital with doctors and nurses around me, not alone with a midwife in the grotty house where I lived. I was scared.

As the birth drew closer, I became more and more anxious. Finally, I felt the baby kicking one morning, and I told Joe to run to the phone box to call the midwife. I gave birth to Jeffrey in August 1958. When I held him for the first time, I felt amazed and overflowing with emotion. He was so tiny and fragile. But this feeling was quickly replaced by shock. How was I going to cope? What was I supposed to do? One minute I was a carefree young woman, but now I was a mother with responsibilities.

I soon realized that Joe didn't have a clue about looking after a baby either. Nor did he seem interested. When we went to the baby shop on Kilburn High Road, he resented having to spend money on a pram and other baby things.

Caring for a baby twenty-four hours a day was hard work. I had to wash the towelling nappies by hand and then hang them on the washing line in the garden or, if it was raining, put them on the clothes horse in front of the fire. As we had no hot water in the flat, I had to boil a saucepan on the gas stove. I found it exhausting getting up in the middle of the night to feed him. Like most mothers, I learnt to be a parent through practice. Once Jeffrey was a few months old, I started taking him with me to see my mum. It was a long journey, involving two Tube trains and a bus. Sometimes my mum came over to Kilburn.

Life became really tough: apart from living in an awful house and having to cope with Joe's moods, I had very little money. The money Joe gave me on a Friday evening never lasted the week. He was very tight. So I got some work cleaning houses for posh families in Fortune Green and I worked as a dinner lady at a secondary school.

By now, Joe and I had settled into what you might call mutual misery. Joe rarely expressed his feelings. He also didn't like neighbours calling round to see us. I think he thought if he became too friendly with them, they would be in the flat all the time.

Despite the difficulties between Joe and me, I always thought I'd have another child. In early 1960 I discovered that I was pregnant again, and in September Carol was born. She didn't begin walking until she was fourteen months old. Then we discovered that one leg was longer than the other and that she had a dislocated hip. She was admitted to Paddington Green Children's Hospital, where she had a traction placed on her leg to pull it back down; and she was kept in for several weeks. She had a plaster placed on both her legs and had to keep it on for about eighteen months— it was called a frog plaster. She was unable to walk in it.

With two children, the accommodation became very cramped. All four of us slept in the same room. When the doctor called one day he remarked that it was like a dormitory.

To bring in extra money I got a job at the offices of Gamba, a ballet-shoe manufacturer, in Soho. I earned twelve pounds a week, more than Joe, but I only stuck it for nine months, as I found working full-time and bringing up the kids in such an awful house was too much. Instead I did some work from home, sprinkling greetings cards with glitter. This has to be the worst job I ever did. The glitter ended up everywhere, even in the children's hair.

I was doing the washing one morning when I heard someone rattling loudly at the door. I rushed downstairs to find a neighbour standing there. She told me a car had hit Jeffrey. I rushed downstairs and out into the street, where I found Jeffrey lying motionless behind a wall, silent in shock. I knelt down beside him and shouted for someone to call an ambulance. It later emerged that the son of the owner of a small workshop had been moving a car and when he put his foot on the accelerator it shot forward, smashing into a wall behind which Jeffrey was playing. When the ambulance arrived, I travelled in the back with him to St John and Elizabeth Hospital in St John's Wood. The doctors examined him and discovered he had broken his thigh. One of them told me it could have been worse. Jeffrey was put in a plaster from below his knee to his chest and kept there for eight weeks.

In 1963 Stella was born. There were five of us in the flat and we were living on top of each other. Joe and I were arguing more and more. It was a desperate situation, but there seemed no way out. When I used to visit my sister Pam in Stevenage, I always came away feeling envious of the kind of lifestyle she had. It seemed so idyllic.

Life wasn't austere as it had been during the war. There was no shortage of food in the shops. And people now started going on holiday. In the summer we took the kids to Whitstable in Kent, where we'd stay in a caravan or chalet. When I was expecting Carol we had been for a week to Warner's holiday camp. When Joe bought a small car, it made it much easier to visit my mum and dad.

Joe was working shifts as a bus driver and he started coming home late. I began to get suspicious. One evening, I said to him, 'Are you seeing someone else?'

'What do you mean?'

'Well, why are you coming home late all the time? Is there another woman?'

'Yeah. So what?'

I picked up a fork off the table and threw it at him. He leapt back as it hit him in the arm.

'What do you think you're playing at? What about me and the children?' I shouted and ran into the bedroom, slamming the door behind me and flinging myself down on the bed, sobbing. There I was looking after the children, struggling to get by on a few pounds a week, and he was running around with another woman. It wasn't fair.

It turned out the woman Joe was seeing was a bus conductor. The following week, he packed a couple of bags and moved out.

I went to the social security office to seek help and soon after they sent someone to visit me. He asked me how much money Joe gave me each week. When I told him that it was just a few pounds, he said: 'Is that all? Does he think that's enough to feed three children?'

I felt angry and resentful towards Joe. But him not being there made little difference because I'd always been the one who had got the children dressed, taken Jeffrey to school, gone shopping and done all the cooking and cleaning. I even had to take heavy bags of washing to the municipal baths. My neighbour next door used to look after the children when I went there; and when she went, I'd look after hers.

Joe came home after a couple of weeks, looking very sheepish. He said he'd made a mistake and that he was sorry.

It never occurred to me not to take him back. In those days, you weren't supposed to give up over something like this. But our marriage didn't get any better and Joe's moods got worse.

I think the main reason I found life so hard was because I felt I had no control over the situation. I had no independence. As time went on, my self-confidence started to disappear. I'd always been very confident, but now I was beginning to doubt whether I had any value. Whatever I said to Joe was never right. I felt he rarely listened to any ideas I had. He made all the decisions in the home and never asked for my opinion.

But in those days you simply stuck at it. The idea of seeking a divorce never entered my mind. I just accepted my situation. I was very miserable, but I didn't moan about it to anyone. There was no point.

One evening when I came home from a part-time job I had got at a tinfoil factory in Park Royal, the faces of Charlie and Buster, whom I had met with Doreen, popped up on the TV. They had been charged with robbing a mail train. They were two members of the gang behind what became known as the Great Train Robbery. To be honest, I wasn't that surprised.

We put our names on the Greater London Council (GLC) housing list. I didn't think there was any point in applying to Hampstead Borough for housing, as it didn't provide much social housing, and any properties it did have always seemed to be given to people living at the other end of the borough. When a housing officer came to visit us and saw the conditions we were living in, he immediately declared the house unfit for human habitation.

Soon after this, a letter arrived from the GLC saying that we were being offered a two-bedroomed flat in a new tower block in Battersea. At that time in London, lots of people were being rehoused in tower blocks. I couldn't believe it! A few days later I went to view it. It was on the sixteenth floor of Selworthy House, just by Battersea Bridge. It had a lovely fitted kitchen that was very light, and a small balcony. When we left, I felt happier than I had done for a long time. I was finally going to escape that awful place in Kilburn. But I could never have guessed exactly how the move to Battersea would change my life forever.

3. Single Parent

I LEANED OVER THE BALCONY, looking at the trees of Battersea Park and beyond it the Thames, and the traffic making its way over Albert Bridge. It was December 1965. Fingering my wedding ring, I told myself this was a new beginning, and that perhaps Joe and I would be able to overcome the difficulties in our marriage. Maybe we could find again whatever it was that attracted us to each other in the first place.

Another reason I was so glad to be living in Battersea was that my sister Vera lived there. In Kilburn I had found it hard being so far away from all my family.

We soon settled into our new home and I found places for the children at a nearby primary school. The only disadvantage to the flat was that it was much more expensive than the house in Kilburn, where we had a controlled rent. Instead of ten shillings a week, we were now paying over four pounds. Joe said that I'd need to get a job to bring in more money. So I found an evening cleaning job in the offices at Morgan's carbon factory. It was filthy work.

One evening when Joe came home from delivering coal in Thornton Heath, he told me that he had a pain in his back. It was unusual for him to be ill. He was a very fit man. The next day, he went to see the doctor, who told him he'd probably pulled a muscle. But a few days later, he could barely move his arms.

On Easter Sunday I was in the kitchen preparing lunch. Joe had gone to the pub for a drink. Suddenly I heard a loud banging on the door. Opening it, I found one of Joe's friends from the pub standing there, breathless.

'Margaret! Joe's been taken to hospital!' he gasped.

'What!'

He explained that Joe had been feeling unwell, so his friends had taken him to Battersea General Hospital for a check-up. He was kept in overnight because he had a high temperature. But the next morning he had become paralysed, so he was taken by ambulance to Stoke Mandeville Hospital, at Aylesbury in Buckinghamshire, to have an operation.

The following day I travelled there with some of his friends to see him. When I arrived on the ward, a doctor took me aside and told me that Joe had an abscess inside his spine.

'What does this mean?' I asked.

He paused and said, 'It means that he will be paralysed for the rest of his life.'

I couldn't take this in. Joe was twenty-nine. I was twenty-eight. We had three children. What were we going to do? How did I explain this to the children?

When I left the hospital I was in a daze. My mind was racing. I couldn't imagine the implications of what the doctor had told me. Once I had come to terms with what had happened to Joe, I began to wonder how I would be able to look after him properly when he came home. How would I manage a wheelchair? How would I cope long-term?

I carried on with my usual routine of getting the children ready for school, cooking, washing and shopping. The shock of what had happened was so great that I didn't think straight. A few days later, I was standing in Sainsbury's in Battersea when I burst into tears. I didn't know how I was going to cope looking after the kids on my own. It was a case of simply getting on with it. I had to give up my cleaning job in the carbon factory because there was no one to look after the children, and claim supplementary benefit.

Suddenly, our marriage was turned upside down. I was now in control and Joe was dependent on me. I used to visit him once in the week and on Saturday. This first meant taking the children to Carshalton for Mum and Dad to look after, or to my sister Vera's. With Stoke Mandeville being so far away, it made for a very long and exhausting day.

One Saturday when I was sitting at his bedside his face suddenly went ashen and then blue.

'Help!' I screamed.

A nurse rushed in, and as soon as she saw Joe, she shouted for a doctor. Several specialists arrived and began pumping his heart. It turned out that Joe had suffered a pulmonary embolism and had nearly died.

He was kept in Stoke Mandeville for several months. The staff were wonderful. They tried to help the patients rebuild their lives and give them hope. Joe became calmer. I think he found something comforting about being in hospital. He enjoyed watching England beat Germany in the World Cup Final, as quite a few of the staff were German.

When I was told that Joe would be returning home, I was terrified. I didn't know how I'd manage to look after the children and him as well. The flat was small and not suitable for a wheelchair, as it was so high up. The hospital arranged for a bed with a pulley to be installed.

In August Joe arrived in an ambulance. When he was wheeled into the flat I can remember thinking how huge the wheelchair looked. It didn't seem that big in the hospital. It was chrome with burgundy leather and had sides and leg pieces that could be detached.

Joe was totally dependent on me. I had to get him up each morning, wash him, take him to the loo and dress him. I had to get up in the night to turn him over in bed. I soon forgot what a full night's sleep felt like. I had hardly any spare time. Caring for three young children and for Joe was exhausting. Stella was two, Carol was five and Jeffrey was seven.

While my family were a great support, Joe's family, who were comfortably off, were hopeless. They hardly ever came to see him and never offered any help with the children. But, in fact, it was the children who kept me going. They just seemed to accept that Joe couldn't walk. They had great fun sitting in his wheelchair and going in and out of the rooms in it.

I was determined to make sure that had what they needed, but my money would only stretch so far. In those days, you couldn't just apply for a credit card when you hit hard times. I remember Carol going to school with a hole in her vest. When she got undressed for PE one of the other girls said to her, 'Tell your mum you can buy a new one in Marks and Spencer.' When she told me this I was filled with shame and sadness that she had been humiliated.

I desperately wanted to get out of this poverty trap, just living from one giro cheque to another, but I didn't know what I could do. The money I received from social security wasn't a lot but it was more than I had ever received from Joe. Apart from supplementary benefit, we received attendance allowance, a heating allowance and laundry allowance. I could now afford to buy a pair of tights, whereas previously I had had to ask Joe for the money.

Joe spent most of his time reading or watching horse racing on TV. The first time I took him out in the wheelchair was nerve-racking. As I wheeled him to Battersea Park, I was worried that he might fall out or that I might lose control. In those days there were no ramps on the pavement. But living on the sixteenth floor of a tower block meant that if the lift wasn't working he couldn't go for his regular treatment to Stoke Mandeville—or anywhere else.

I never felt really settled in Battersea, as I knew that we would have to move at some point because the flat was unsuitable for Joe. The council told us that we would be moving to a flat on the Stockwell Park Estate, but it fell through. This was to turn out to be a blessing in disguise.

In March 1967 we moved into a flat in Kennington that had been adapted for people with disabilities. Joe was in Stoke Mandeville on the day of the move and my mum looked after Carol and Stella. Jeffrey was a great help in packing everything away. I remember that the removal men left us without putting the beds together. The flat was on the ground floor in a three-storey block on the Brandon Estate, which was a highly acclaimed development near the Walworth Road. It had a ramp and there was more space inside than in Selworthy House. My brother-in-law Eddie made parallel bars for Joe, so that he could exercise. The architects had thought it a good idea to mix young families with older people. But the old people didn't like being surrounded by kids all day.

I needed to find a school for Jeffrey and Carol. The nearest was St Paul's primary. Everyone I spoke to told me it was difficult to get a place there. But I got in because one of the head's children had been to the same primary school as I had in Battersea. I found a part-time place for Stella in the day nursery in nearby Sutherland Square.

When the head teacher asked me if I would be a lunchtime playground helper at the school I agreed. I just had to keep an eye on the kids and make sure they had their lunch.

I soon discovered that the flat had terrible damp, because it had been shoddily built. One morning when I woke up I saw puddles on the tiled floor of the bedroom. Later, I went out and phoned the housing office.

'You do realize that you give off seven pints of water when you breathe at night,' said a housing officer.

This seemed a stupid thing to say, so I replied. 'Well, I've slept in many bedrooms in my time, but I've never woken up with puddles on the floor before.'

A social worker called Dave visited me and got night storage heaters installed. He also arranged for us to go on holiday in the summer with some other families to a centre in Whitstable run by the Shaftesbury Society. Although the accommodation was basic—we slept in Nissen huts—we all had a wonderful time. The staff played rounders and cricket with the kids and took them to the beach so that we had some free time. Because the Shaftesbury Society is a Baptist organization, alcohol wasn't allowed in the centre, so some of us went to a nearby pub. I realized that there were people far worse off than me. One couple were blind and had three boys they couldn't control, while one teenager had multiple sclerosis.

My local GP was Sir Monty Levine, who ran a small surgery near Kennington Tube station. He was also the coroner for Southwark and the GP for Jim Callaghan, the Prime Minister. He had a large handlebar moustache. He always wore a white linen jacket and had holes in his socks. In the summer he wore a panama hat. I could imagine him at public school, with his shirt tails hanging out. He ran the surgery with his wife. She looked very angular and was far more formal than him. After he was knighted she would call out, 'Margaret Prosser for Lady Levine.'

Dr Monty often called on me at home to see how I was coping. He drove a Wolseley. Once, during the school holidays, he brought his daughter with him and she and Stella played the recorder together.

Because Joe regularly developed kidney infections, Dr Monty decided it would be best if he had his bladder removed and was given a urostomy bag. Joe found this very hard to take.

One day when Dr Monty called, he asked, 'Do you ever get depressed, Margaret?'

'I haven't time to get depressed. There are so many things to do.'

He burst out laughing.

But it was true. I didn't have any time to mope about. But, deep down, I must have been depressed. It was just that I suppressed these feelings. Joe and I spoke very little. He spent most of his time sitting in the chair reading. I took him to the library most weeks.

Kennington was a close-knit community. The estate, like many council estates in those days, had a resident caretaker who looked after the flower beds, made sure the rubbish chute wasn't blocked and told off the kids if they were misbehaving. In those days you didn't hear about muggings or robberies. I remember how shocked everyone was when an old man who delivered the newspapers was murdered.

I did most of my shopping on the Walworth Road, which in those days was what I call brassy working-class. The men used to get good wages from working at the docks or in printing. I used to buy broderie anglaise trimmed dress material and velvet ribbon from a haberdashery stall so that I could make dresses for Carol and Stella. East Street market was fantastic for fruit and veg. The Co-op department store on Camberwell New Road never seemed to have anything in it. If you went to buy a pair of knitting needles, they never seemed to have the size you wanted. Sometimes I caught the bus to Brixton, which had the Bon Marché department store, or Streatham, which had Pratt's. Both shops were part of John Lewis.

That Christmas, Joe's parents came to visit us. I found it quite difficult to be festive and jolly. When his dad had too much to drink he became nasty. Mind you, there was an amusing moment when he insisted on pouring so much brandy over the Christmas pudding that it collapsed.

My dad came over sometimes to take the children to Carshalton for the weekend. He always arrived with an empty suitcase for their clothes. The kids enjoyed it and it gave me some time to myself. He was working part-time as a porter at St Helier Hospital and we nicknamed him 'Dr

Kildare', because by the way he talked it seemed as though he was responsible for running the hospital.

At that time, the day centres run by Southwark Council only catered for elderly people, not younger people with disabilities. Joe used to attend a day centre on the other side of Camberwell, but he found it depressing because everyone else was so much older. The rights of disabled people were only beginning to be addressed back then.

'I don't like going there. I'm not interested in bingo or the other things they do,' he said.

When Dave called to see me the next day, I said, 'I think there's a need for a centre for younger disabled people. Young people don't want to sit in a centre with old people.'

'I agree,' he said, and then explained that Southwark Council was building a new centre at Otto Street, but this was only going to serve older people.

'Why doesn't the council provide something?'

'Well, why don't you start a campaign?'

'What? Me?' I'd never been involved in any campaigns and didn't have a clue how you would go about starting one.

He said he'd take me to the Community Development Project in Braganza Street and the people there would help me to lobby Southwark to provide a facility for younger people. I thought, OK, but I wasn't sure what I might be letting myself in for. The project was part of a national programme that had been set up by the Home Office following Enoch Powell's 'rivers of blood' speech in 1968. Its aim was gather information about the impact of social policies and services and to encourage co-ordination and self-help. CDPs were set up in areas of high social deprivation, and employed professional community workers and researchers.

The following week, he took me to meet several community workers. When I explained what I wanted to do, they all agreed to help me. The community workers knew how the council worked. They knew the key councillors and all about council committee meetings and procedures.

We identified the numbers of young disabled people in the borough who used day centres and then got a group of disabled and able-bodied people together. CDP managed to get the issue on the social services agenda. A few months later, Southwark agreed to provide a day centre for young people in Otto Street. When it opened, we held a party at CDP.

I enjoyed the campaign, especially working with people who wanted to make the local area a better place. After the success of the campaign, Dave asked me if I wanted to get involved with the Child Poverty Action Group, which was based at a place called Blackfriars Settlement. I thought to myself, why not? It would provide me with an interest.

The following week, I found myself sitting in a circle in a large room with about twenty social and community workers. Dave introduced me and explained how I had campaigned for the day centre. Everyone smiled and told me I was very welcome.

I sat there listening to the group discussing various local issues. When someone said how terrible it was that there had been criticisms of a woman who had bought some expensive shoes for her son and didn't have enough money left for food, everyone else nodded in agreement. But I sat there thinking, the woman must be stupid to spend money on posh shoes instead of food.

When the group decided to try and identify the opticians in Southwark who would provide glasses on the NHS, I volunteered to carry out a survey. I'd never done anything like this before, but I wanted to get more involved in things.

Over the next couple of weeks, I travelled around the borough, hopping on and off buses, and visiting opticians.

I pretended that one of my children needed glasses and asked if they provided them under the NHS. I enjoyed the experience and wrote a brief report and took it with me to the next meeting. When I handed it to one of the community workers, I felt very pleased with myself.

In 1971 the government conducted a census. When I sat down at the table in the living room to complete it one night, one of the questions pulled me up. How many O levels did I have? I had none, but my nephew, who had been to a grammar school in Stevenage, had ten. When I thought about the fact that here I was, at thirty-five years of age and with no qualifications, I felt I had missed out.

So I decided to attend evening classes at Peckham Girls' School in Peckham Road. I studied O levels in English language and the history of parliament. Sitting behind a desk in a classroom again seemed strange. The other students were a mixture of ages. There were several black women. I was relieved to see that I wasn't the oldest person there.

I found doing the reading and writing essays hard work, but I really enjoyed the classes. However, Joe couldn't understand why I wanted to study again.

'It's not going to get you anywhere,' he said.

'It doesn't matter whether it gets me anywhere. Education has a value in itself,' I said.

He didn't reply, but I could tell he didn't like the idea that I was doing something for myself for a change.

The following year, I studied English literature and modern history. When my exam results arrived, I was over the moon that I had passed. Although Joe seemed unimpressed, my kids and my mum and dad were really happy for me.

In 1972 Alan Davies, the director at CDP, asked me if I would cover the advice desk at lunchtime. He said that because I had a good working knowledge of the social security system I would be able to deal with most of the queries. If

I couldn't deal with the problem, then I was to make a note of it and pass the details on to a community worker. I was paid £4 per week, which was the amount I was allowed to earn without it affecting my supplementary benefit.

The advice centre was located in the front of the shop. It was kitted out with second-hand furniture, which made it seem very tatty. At the back were two offices staffed by secretaries, and a kitchen. Upstairs were offices for the researchers and director. I thought most of the people there dressed very scruffily, and wondered if they were doing this because they wanted to be seen as more like the working class. But most of the people who came to see us always dressed up. The centre was open five days a week. Anyone could just turn up. You didn't need an appointment.

Most of the problems people came with were to do with housing, not social security. I remember one woman who lived in Stoney Buildings, which were scheduled for demolition, complaining that her flat was unfit and saying to me, 'I can sit on my toilet and lean forward and turn the oven down.'

I also remember the mother of two boys caught stealing from a shop in Camberwell asking the magistrate if they could keep the alarm clock because they didn't have one.

When I attended a public meeting about squatters held at St Paul's church hall. I was surprised that all the social workers supported squatting. I didn't believe that anyone had the right to just walk into a property and live there. So I stood up and said, 'It's not fair that people should be allowed to squat in council properties. There are families who have been on the waiting list for ages.' All eyes turned to me. I think they all thought I was some sort of raving right-winger. But then other locals in the hall started agreeing with me. It felt good.

The council had moved all sorts of problem families into the area because, it was thought at the time, the houses only had a short life. I had never met people like them before, despite having spent most of my life living on a council estate.

In 1973 I received a phone call from my sister Pam to say that my dad had died. He had developed a brain tumour, fallen over in the bathroom and been rushed to hospital. I visited him several times, but he died within a few weeks. I felt very sad, because he hadn't had much of a retirement. He was really enjoying life, going on outings and to pensioners' clubs. He was seventy-two.

Joe wasn't interested in what I was doing. Once, when I came back after taking Carol to the pictures, he was very upset and angry. He'd phoned his mum to say that he'd been left alone and felt deserted. I could understand this, but he also said he wasn't being properly looked after, which wasn't true.

The next day, his mum phoned and accused me of neglecting him. The irony was that she never came to visit him. They were much better off than my parents and they even had a car. I was very upset. I decided after this that I couldn't cope with the situation any more. I felt that Joe didn't appreciate me. I did everything for him, but he never thanked me. When his family accused me of not looking after him, that was the last straw. Eventually I went to see Dr Monty, who said he would visit us at home. When he turned up, Joe wasn't very talkative and just complained that he was on his own in the evenings. This wasn't true. I was with him nearly every evening.

Dr Monty arranged for a psychiatrist to visit me at home. I knew that he had suggested this in order to be able to produce a report saying I couldn't cope. When I tried to tell him how I was feeling I kept bursting into tears. I felt that I'd collapsed inside.

One morning Joe said to me, 'We'll all be better off if I go into hospital.'

'What do you mean?'

'I'll have more people to talk to. I'll be much better off.'

I didn't say anything, but I felt annoyed with him. Why did he think he wasn't being looked after already? I did everything for him. I felt he was very ungrateful.

We explained what was happening to the children. I think they could see that things were not good between Joe and me. Children are very resilient. I believe that as long as kids have some certainty in their lives and their routine remains more or less the same, they can cope with these sorts of situations.

Dr Monty and the psychiatrist arranged for him to be admitted to a hospital in Stockwell in June 1974. When the ambulance arrived for Joe a few days later, and I watched him being lifted into the back, I felt a mixture of sadness and anger. I didn't feel guilty over him going into care, but I think that some people might have expected me to. I felt that I'd done all I could for him for eight-and-a-half years. Our marriage had really started to fall apart from day one. We'd had a whirlwind romance and I'd got pregnant as a result, and we thought getting married was the natural thing to do. But we were both too young to realize what we were getting into.

After Joe had left, I started receiving phone calls in the middle of the night. When I picked up the receiver, the person at the other end hung up. It was very scary and creepy. I knew it was Joe's dad. He wanted to find out if I had another man. His mother phoned several times but each time I hung up. I couldn't bring myself to speak to her after what she had said.

I received a birthday card from Joe—the first one I'd ever received in our sixteen years of marriage. Two weeks later he phoned to say he wanted to come home. I told him I didn't want him back. I felt really let down by him for not taking my side against his mother. I'd done everything for him for all those years. I'd got up in the middle of the night, washed him, dressed him, cooked for him and taken him out. I never once felt he was grateful or ever gave me a second thought.

After a few weeks in the hospital in Stockwell, Joe was transferred to the Queen Elizabeth Hospital in Walton on Thames. Carol and Stella used to visit him, but Jeffrey refused to. Joe had constantly criticized him. I don't ever remember him praising him. I think Joe was resentful that Jeffrey had so much life and energy and he didn't. While I could understand Joe's feelings, I couldn't understand why he wanted to humiliate his own son.

I had now found a new lease of life. I was working, studying and also acting as a member of the PTA at St Paul's school. I travelled overseas for the first time when I helped escort a group of kids from problem families to Ostend. Once they had got off the ferry, I returned to Dover.

Part of me was relieved that Joe had gone into care. But another part of me was worried about how I was going to cope financially. The extra social security payments we received because he was disabled were taken away and I was put on the short-term benefit rate. So I lost attendance allowance, laundry and heating allowance and the long-term allowance. I was determined to come off benefits and find a full-time job somewhere. But where?

4. Back to School

I'D ENJOYED MY WORK at the CDP and didn't want to leave. But I would have to, as I needed a full-time job. I told this to Alan Davies, the director.

'Look, if you can hold on until October when the council meets again, we're going to ask for our grant to be restructured,' he said.

'Oh.' I wasn't sure what he meant.

'Yes, if they agree we are going to create an advice centre organizer post. And I think you would stand a good chance of getting it.'

Southwark Council did agree to restructure the CDP's funding, and a new post was created. I applied for it and was successful. I couldn't believe that I now had a full-time job doing something I really wanted to do.

The CDP was split into an action team and a research team, and employed community workers, a schools worker and a planning officer who had been seconded from Southwark Council. I was part of the action team. Apart from dealing with the problems of clients, my responsibilities included making sure all our information was up to date, producing fact sheets and publicity, and managing two part-time members of staff.

I was shocked that many of the people who came to see me seemed incapable of organizing their lives. Many of the kids never went to school. I couldn't understand it. I'd grown up on a council estate, but everyone I knew had self-respect and could take care of their families.

We worked with tenants' groups and set up playgroups and youth clubs. Most of the families in Walworth were white, while in Peckham there were more black families.

In the early 1970s, under a national Home Office programme, local authorities across London were pulling down slums. Properties that were falling apart and didn't have bathrooms or indoor toilets were being replaced by blocks of flats, both low-rise and high-rise. In Southwark, two huge estates were being built near the Elephant and Castle, the Heygate and the Aylesbury. The original plan was to link the Heygate Estate with the Aylesbury and North Peckham Estates by a series of walkways, so you wouldn't have to use the pavements. This never happened, which was a good thing, as these estates became notorious for crime.

Many residents were being moved out to other areas. Southwark had planned to pull down all the houses in Doddington Grove. On one side of the street there was a row of about twenty four-bedroomed houses, which were all in good condition. When the residents refused to move, the CDP took up their case and the council eventually agreed to let the houses remain.

For some people, living on an estate was a good thing, but at the same time large estates with walkways were not the solution to the housing problem. For example, one of the problems with the Aylesbury was that it had lots of paths that didn't go anywhere. You could find yourself walking along a path thinking it was going to take you out of the estate and then come to a concrete wall. Another problem was that the walkways ran over the bedrooms of the flats below, which created a noise problem. Estates also led to people not looking after their homes. People who had polished their door knockers and cleaned their steps began throwing rubbish over the balconies of flats on the Heygate. This was an example of 'defensible space'. No one owned the space below, so nobody cared about it.

A group of shopkeepers on Manor Place came to us and claimed that what Southwark was offering under compulsory purchase orders was too low. John Hobson, our community lawyer, told me afterwards that for years they had sent in tax returns with figures much lower than what they really earned. So when the council valued their businesses they based the valuations on the income they had declared.

Colin Roberts, a researcher, saw potential in me, so when he took me in his pale blue Volkswagen Beetle to visit community projects in other parts of the country, he would give me mini political lectures. Colin was a member of the Communist Party and dedicated to community politics. If he said he was going to do something, he always did it. People often think of Communism as being radical, but it could be quite conservative. Correct behaviour and discipline mattered a lot to Communists.

He told me that Southwark Council thought the CDP would be another arm of social services. Instead it had turned out to be a radical organization that was trying to give people the power and knowledge necessary to bring about changes in the local community. It was only later I realized that I gave the project an air of legitimacy because I was a local working-class woman from a council estate who had gone on to do quite well.

In 1975 the CDP, together with Southwark Council for Voluntary Service, the umbrella organization for voluntary groups in the borough, began a campaign to open a law centre in Southwark. There were so many residents coming to us for advice that John Hobson was struggling to cope with the workload. The CDP lobbied the Home Office and a group of civil servants came to visit us and assess us for a grant. The Home Office had devised a research method to measure social deprivation.

One of the officials told me that they didn't usually leave their office to see the public projects seeking funding. I was amazed when I heard this. How could they properly assess a project unless they went to see it?

Revd David Gerard, the vicar of St Paul's, the nearby Anglican church, was very involved with the CDP and local

tenants' associations. He and his wife lived with their four
kids in the vicarage. He'd been educated at Oxford and saw
his mission as working with what he regarded as the poor.
When he first arrived in the parish, he was quoted in the
Evening Standard as saying, 'I'm going to Walworth, the
home of boxers and gangsters.' This didn't go down well
with most of the locals. I helped him to produce the parish
newsletter. Each month, Stella and I would paste text on to
sheets of paper and then take them on the train to the printer
in Rochester.

David said to me one day, 'You know, if you want to get
things done, you should join the local Labour Party.'

'I hadn't thought of that,' I said. I knew many people at
the CDP were members of the Labour Party, but it had never
crossed my mind to join.

He gave me an application form and I sent it off. When
I received my membership card a couple of weeks later, I
decided to attend the monthly meeting of the Newington
ward at the Labour Party offices on Walworth Road. I
arrived to find a scruffy office with brown and cream walls
and several elderly men and women sitting on worn chairs
that didn't match. I can't remember what was discussed at
the meeting, but I do remember that it was very dull—not at
all what I'd expected. I quickly learnt in my first few meetings
that no one had any ideas about what the party could do at
a local level. I also learnt that the local councillors were
happy with this, as it meant that they could do what they
wanted. Had I not been so idealistic, I would probably have
quit. But I didn't. Something told me that David was right,
and that by being involved with local politics you could
change things. Colin and Linda, his partner, and others I
knew who were involved in local politics told me that I
could change things, although they didn't tell me how.

I was now discovering a new lease of life. I no longer felt
depressed and that my life wasn't going anywhere. I was

becoming a different person. I started going out with people from the CDP to wine bars or to the pub. I changed the way I dressed. I now wore jeans and desert boots and a velvet jacket I bought in a jumble sale. But my phase of dressing down didn't last for long. Everyone along the Old Kent Road always dressed up.

I started to read more widely, especially about politics. I read books such as *Down and Out in Paris and London* and *Homage to Catalonia* by George Orwell, a biography of a former leader of the Communist party in Spain, and the writings of the political activist Angela Davies. I also read about the Black Power movement in the United States. For my fortieth birthday, Colin Roberts bought me a book about the working class in London in the nineteenth century. We laughed about this later, as it was a very depressing book, and not the kind of thing to lift your spirits when you hit forty.

But, despite my new knowledge, I lacked confidence and was unsure of myself. When I attended a CDP conference in Warwick with Colin and several other staff, I was very conscious that everyone else there was very middle-class and assured. I think Colin sensed this.

'Don't worry about it, Margaret,' he said.

'But they all seem so well educated.'

'Well, you know things they don't know.'

That might have been true, but I felt I needed to learn and understand more. All these people at the conference had been to university and seemed so self-assured. This only served to make me feel less confident.

One day not long after I had started at the CDP, Alan said, 'Margaret, you have lots of practical knowledge about advice and politics, but you don't have much theory.'

Soon after, he came into the office one morning, holding open a copy of a social-work magazine and pointing to an advert for a part-time postgraduate course in advice and information studies at North-East London Polytechnic in Stratford. 'This is for you,' he said.

It sounded right up my street, so I applied and was called for an interview. Because I didn't have a degree, I was asked to write an essay. This wasn't too hard, as I had been used to essay-writing on my O level courses.

The course, which had been established by the Citizens Advice Bureau (CAB), involved attending classes twice a week. Most of the other students were women working for the CAB, and they seemed more educated than I was. Jean Donaldson, a well-known sociologist, was one of my lecturers and Tessa Jowell, who was then chair of social services at Camden Council, came and gave a talk on one occasion. I had a lot of reading to do for the course, and spent Sunday afternoons hunched over books at the kitchen table. I had to write essays about housing, social security, interviews and social law. I didn't feel I had that much in common with most of the other students. I saw myself as a radical.

I found the course stretched my mind and changed the way I thought about things. It provided me with a framework to understand the work I was doing. And I started to see how important it was that ordinary people were listened to when decisions were being made. As part of the course, I did a two-week placement at Balham Law Centre, which was useful in enabling me to look at other ways of handling cases.

I recognized that the children were having to deal with some big changes in their lives. Joe was no longer at home and I was working full-time. I needed to make sure I was there for them. Stella was still at primary school, and she came to the CDP after school and would help me, putting up posters on the walls and windows and tidying up the sewing materials and pens and paper in the truancy project, which used one of the rooms in the building.

In October 1974 we had to leave the flat in Kennington because Joe was no longer living at home and the council needed it for someone who had a disability. We moved into a three-bedroom GLC flat on Wynham Road in Camberwell. The flat was ideal because it was in the same street as Archbishop Michael Ramsey School, which Carol attended. I remember one of the teachers saying to me, 'I'd never send my kids to this school.' I thought this was an outrageous thing to say.

But many schools in Southwark were very poor, which meant the good ones were oversubscribed. I got to know some of the teachers, and I wasn't that impressed by them. As soon as school ended they would be in the pub across the road. One night a teacher was so drunk she couldn't find her way home and ended up sleeping in someone's doorway.

When Harvey Hinds—the chair of the Inner London Education Authority (ILEA), which was part of the GLC—and the head of Vauxhall Girls' School wrote a series of articles in *The Guardian*, praising comprehensive schools, I wrote a letter to the same paper saying that, if comprehensive schools were so wonderful, why did they send their children to Mary Datchelor Girls' School in Camberwell?

I helped to organize a group of parents to go to County Hall, the home of the ILEA, to make their views known to Harvey Hinds. The GLC seemed a very distant organization. As an ordinary person you didn't feel you could influence its decisions in any way. So one afternoon we turned up and marched down a series of long corridors to his office. When we found it, we walked straight in without knocking. Hinds, who was sitting behind a desk, looked startled and very nervous. We stood there, demanding he do something to improve the borough's schools. He did his best to try and appear concerned, agreeing with what we said, but without promising anything. After we'd said our piece, we marched back out again. I heard that on another occasion a group of mums had chased him down the corridor.

I'd began to go walking some weekends with Barbara Whitehead, a PE teacher from Archbishop Michael Ramsey

School, and her husband. We went camping in Wales, where I climbed Snowdon, the highest mountain in Wales, and Cadair Idris. What I remember most about climbing Cadair Idris was that you hauled yourself up the mountainside and then saw the summit. But it wasn't the summit. It was a plateau with a large lake, so you still had a long climb ahead. I found climbing mountains exhilarating. Despite it being arduous, I loved it.

The longest walk I've ever done was the Lyke Wake, a 42-mile hike through the North Yorkshire countryside, which has to be done in a day. Colin and Linda, who worked as a researcher for TASS, the white-collar engineering union, came up with the idea. We practised by walking from Camberwell to Bermondsey and also around the perimeter of Hyde Park, which is five miles long. After doing two circuits we used to crash out in the flat of David Triesman, a friend of Colin's, who later became chairman of the Football Association and a peer.

Jeffrey decided to come with us on the walk, as he knew Colin and Linda and some of those who played for Southwark Strollers, a cricket team for people working for voluntary organizations. During Whitsun weekend in 1977 about twenty of us drove to North Yorkshire in a convoy of cars. Everyone was either a member of the Labour Party or the Communist Party or a lawyer. We decided to call ourselves the Red Ramblers.

We set off from the pub in Osmotherly at 4.00 a.m. and walked in seven-mile stretches. At each point there was a support group handing out water, bananas, dates and clean socks. This was the first time I'd been this far north in England. I can remember walking over the brow of a hill and seeing Middlesbrough below. It was still a steel town then. An extraordinary pall of orange gas hung over it. When we walked past RAF Fylingdales, some of the Communist members started talking about how we were all being spied on.

As we trudged over the moors we talked about current affairs and history and sang songs from the shows we knew. There was optimism among those on the left in the 1970s because the workers were seen to have power. I was amazed at how clever so many of the group were. Michael Siefert, for example, a Jewish lawyer and a Communist, could talk about art, theatre, history, anything you care to name.

As we were clambering over some rocks, Jeffrey turned and said to me, 'You're a complete sell-out, Mum.'

'What do you mean?' His outburst surprised me.

'Your politics are rubbish.'

Jeffrey had started getting involved in politics when he went to Southwark College and became president of the student union and organized sit-ins. He had joined the Socialist Workers' Party, which was very Trotskyite. While I saw myself as a radical, he thought I was too conventional. Jeffrey hadn't been interested in reading at school. But now, like me, he was devouring books and expanding his knowledge and understanding.

The walk ended at Robin Hood's Bay and took nearly fourteen hours. Each of us was given a certificate and a cloth badge—in the shape of a coffin! We then drove to a hotel in Scarborough, looking forward to a drink. But the hotel turned out to be teetotal. We all found it hilarious that Linda, of all people, had booked us into a teetotal hotel. So, after a long bath and a change of clothes, we set off in search of a pub. The walk was so enjoyable that a group of us decided to go on walks together each year and later went to Ireland, Scotland and Wales.

I found myself getting more and more interested in employment rights and the role of the unions, so in August 1976, when workers at Grunwick, a film-processing company in Neasden, went on strike over union recognition, Colin and I decided to join them on the picket line. The majority of the strikers, mainly Asian women, weren't union members, but they were supported by the Association of Professional, Executive, Clerical and Computer Staff (APEX). Grunwick became known as 'the Ascot of the Left' because trade-union activists from all over the country travelled there to lend their support.

Among the pickets were Harriet Harman and Jack Dromey, who both worked at Brent Law Centre, which had organized the demonstration after a group of women workers went there to ask what their rights were. I had met them a few months earlier at a law centre conference. On the picket line, I also met Maureen Donnelly, who was active in the BT managers' union. She asked to travel with us from Camberwell and went on to become a good friend.

Colin and I went to Grunwick several times. I found standing on the picket line incredibly exciting. There was an amazing buzz. On one occasion, I was asked to hold a miners' banner while the miners raced off down the street to try and stop workers entering the factory or join in a scuffle. When the police arrested people, we wrote down their names and the numbers on the epaulettes of the police officers.

The CDP was reaching the end of its funding and there was uncertainty about its future. So, in the summer of 1977, I left and went to work as an advice worker at the Southwark Law Project, where Colin and John were also now working. I was feeling more confident and even more committed to do what I could to help people improve their lives.

5. Making a Difference

THE SOUTHWARK LAW PROJECT had two offices, one in Bermondsey and another in East Dulwich. I worked in Bermondsey, which was based above a general advice centre in a scruffy building among the shops in Southwark Park Road. We had one large office, which was kitted out with second-hand furniture. If I wanted to take a copy of anything, I had to use the clumsy duplicating machine, which meant I would end up with my hands covered in ink.

Bermondsey seemed a desolate area. It had once been a thriving part of London's docks when ships from all over the world docked just below Tower Bridge, bringing wood, bananas and all sorts of things. But following the closure of the docks in the late 1960s, and with it the closure of most of the factories, it had become run down. On its sprawling council estates on either side of Jamaica Road there was high unemployment and all the usual social problems that go with it. Bermondsey later became a trendy part of London, with restaurants and posh flats, but in those days no one ever went to Bermondsey unless they had to. It didn't have a Tube station then, which made it feel a very isolated part of London.

We operated both a drop-in and an appointment system, and opened late some evenings, so people could visit after work. We also ran a mobile advice shop, which went around the Rotherhithe New Road area.

John Hobson was our senior lawyer. Volunteer lawyers and social workers would help out at the evening sessions. Each of us working at the project had a specialism. Mine was benefits. I dealt mainly with supplementary benefit, sickness benefit, invalidity benefit and attendance allowance. I also handled some housing cases, but if one was complicated I'd ask one of the other members of the team for help. Likewise, if someone had a complex benefit query they would come to me. Under an agreement with the Law Society, we didn't handle conveyancing, or personal injury or criminal cases over a certain value. This was in order to protect the bread-and-butter work of solicitors. We had a rota for evening work. Because I didn't have a partner, I probably worked more evenings than anyone else.

In order to get to know Bermondsey, and to make ourselves known, we went out and met members of the tenants' and residents' associations on the council estates.

The sessions at the Law Project were nearly always busy. Unemployment was high. When I explained to people who had lost their jobs how much unemployment benefit they would receive they were astonished. 'How am I suppose to survive on that?' would be the usual reply. I knew from experience how difficult it would be to live on such a low amount, but there was nothing I could do. So I tried to encourage them in their search for work. Sometimes old ladies who couldn't afford to pay their gas bills because of the standing charge turned up seeking help. Others who came through the door seemed unable to cope with the demands of life and as a result had clocked up rent arrears or other debts. It was common for someone to arrive with a carrier bag stuffed with old bills and letters, which they would spread out on my desk and then launch into lengthy and detailed accounts of why their finances were in a mess.

There were plenty of characters in the area. On one occasion an elderly man came into the office and told me he'd been advised by his doctor to keep taking his tablets.

'What's the problem?' I asked.

He leaned forward and lowered his voice. 'Because people could walk through my wall.'

'Your wall?'

'Yes, I have no privacy whatsoever. So I've done as the doctor told me and taken the tablets.'

'That's good.'

'I put them in my ear.'

'Really.' I sat there, trying to appear serious.

We didn't wear rose-tinted spectacles. We weren't naïve. We all knew that some people who came to us were trying to pull a fast one. There will always be people trying to play the system and milk it for what they could get. One man arrived with a large tax bill and said it was outrageous that he had been asked to pay it. I couldn't help but notice that he was wearing a Rolex watch.

One day, a Filipina nurse came to see me and explained that she'd lost her job and her accommodation in Clapham Common and was staying with friends in Bermondsey. I said I'd do some investigations and asked her to come back the following week. When she arrived, she was clutching a bottle of whisky, which she handed to me. I tried to refuse it, but she insisted I took it. I think she thought this might produce a favourable outcome for her. But it didn't make any difference. I told the other staff about it and we agreed to keep it for when we had an office party.

I told my sister Vera about it. 'But I don't even like whisky.'

She laughed and said, 'You should put an advert in the paper: owner of bottle of whisky wants to meet owner of a bottle of gin.'

Many people were anxious about their benefits and didn't know what they were entitled to. The benefits system was so complicated. People were never told what they might be entitled to, but had to find out for themselves. Quite often someone would walk in waving a letter from the Department of Health and Social Security (as it then was) saying that their rate of benefit had been changed, and demanding to know why. It was very hard when you had to tell someone who was struggling that he or she wasn't entitled to any extra money. I had to say, 'I'm really sorry, but that's the system.' For the very hard up, I applied for grants for cookers, fridges, beds and other essential items. Sometimes, when someone was refused, I appealed at the DHSS tribunal in Lewisham.

I have learnt that no matter what kind of benefits system you have, there will always be a few people who abuse it. So when it's made tighter and tighter, it just becomes more complicated and leads to mistakes being made because no one understands it. You need to try to make sure that people are not receiving benefits they are not entitled to. But you also need to ensure that genuine people are not affected. Far more people miss out on benefits they are entitled to than receive benefits they are not entitled to.

Sometimes we made home visits. One day I went to visit a woman who had a hole in the ceiling of her living room on the top floor of a private rented flat in East Dulwich. Pigeons had begun roosting in it. When she left her flat she had to use her umbrella. After John Hobson threatened Southwark Council with legal action, she was quickly rehoused.

Another time, I remember going to see a woman who worked and also cared for her sick husband to tell her that she had been awarded attendance allowance. Neither her GP nor the social workers had told her that she might be entitled to it. She lived in a poky third-floor flat overlooking the railway line to London Bridge.

'You mean I'll get extra money?' she said.

'Yes. It's not a means-tested benefit.'

Her eyes lit up. 'Oh! You are my angel.'

It was moments like these that made me feel fulfilled in what I was doing. At times, listening to so many stories of hardship and hopelessness was incredibly draining. And dealing with housing cases could be very frustrating as they often dragged on and on. But when I had some good news to give someone I felt that it was all worth it, because I was making a difference.

In order to help the clients, I knew it was important to develop good working relationships with the staff at the local DHSS office. So I attended meetings with the managers to talk about issues and any changes in the system. I went on a number of training courses, including a seminar on housing law run by Nick Raynsford, who became an MP, and a welfare rights course at Morley College.

To handle the kinds of cases we did you needed to be a people person, patient, caring and with an eye for detail. You also had to have a sense of humour if you wanted to stay sane. One of the staff wore a badge that said on one side, 'I have sat here and listened to your story for a considerable period of time.' On the other side it said, 'Now, fuck off.'

Once a week, I also provided benefits advice at our centre in Lordship Lane, East Dulwich, which was run with general advice workers provided by Southwark Council staff. Whereas in Bermondsey I saw mostly families, many of those who came to the centre in East Dulwich were single unemployed men living in rooms and finding it hard to survive on social security. It was even harder for families.

At lunchtime I sometimes went with some of the other staff for a drink at a wine bar around the corner. One afternoon, we decided to go for tea at the Ritz. Colin said he was going to buy a new cricket bat from Lillywhites, so we all decided to go with him. I didn't feel guilty, as I had worked late many evenings and not been paid extra for it. I was amazed at how opulent the Ritz was. But I have to admit that I really enjoyed it.

Local councillors would pop in to see us. While the MP for Dulwich was a regular visitor, the Bermondsey MP, Bob Mellish, didn't want anything to do with us. He saw us as interfering and too left wing. We held regular meetings with the staff from the advice centre below. I thought they were an airy-fairy bunch who were better at talking than doing anything.

One of my jobs was to represent clients at social security tribunals, which were held in Lewisham. A typical case might be that of a parent refused money to buy a school uniform for a child. The room tribunals were held in always seemed dark and sombre. I felt that the people who sat on tribunals looked down on the people we worked with and didn't understand the kind of difficulties they found themselves in.

I also represented clients at employment tribunals, which were held at Ebury Bridge Road in Pimlico. The first person I represented was a man called Shirley, not a good name for a black construction worker. When he told me his name, I struggled to keep a straight face, thinking of the Johnny Cash Song, 'A Boy Named Sue'. Shirley claimed he'd been unfairly dismissed. When he was given a card and asked to read the oath, he looked uncomfortable. The chairman of the tribunal glared at him.

I stood up and said, 'I think he finds it difficult to read.'

It was common to find out that someone couldn't read or write. When someone came into the centre, I'd often ask if he or she was used to filling in forms instead of asking directly about reading and writing.

I also did some medical appeals at St Dunstan's House. I always found these very tricky, as you had to speak before a panel of doctors, which was quite intimidating. One time, a Pakistani man who was claiming invalidity benefit and who worked in a bakery claimed that a hot tray of cakes had fallen on his foot and injured it. He blamed his employer. He told me he had injured his other foot after an accident in Kashmir. The doctors became totally confused about which foot was which.

'Which foot are you talking about?'

'The foot that has been injured,' said the man.

'Injured where? At the bakery?'

It was pure comedy.

I attended monthly meetings of the St Giles ward Labour Party, which met in Lansbury House, a run-down building on Camberwell Grove. There were never more than about fifteen members at the meetings, which often dragged on for a couple of hours or more. I thought they needed to be much shorter. So when the chair fell vacant I put my name forward, and I was elected.

It was around this time that Southwark Council introduced a policy of making hard-to-let properties available to young professionals, such as teachers and doctors. Many of them joined the Labour Party and started attending meetings. They were all idealistic, believing that socialism provided the answer to creating a fairer society. They began to overturn decisions made by the old guard and gradually pushed the party membership to the left.

We were quite a radical bunch at the Law Centre. There was a movement in the law sector at that time to establish non-hierarchical workplaces, where all members of staff were paid the same and lawyers would do their own typing. But we didn't agree with it, as it would do away with secretarial jobs, which were very important for local women because they paid well. And we all thought it was ridiculous to waste the expertise of a lawyer on typing.

At a law centres conference I attended in Warwick, at the plenary session members were invited to join a special-interest group: disabled, black or women. Everyone else—in other words, the white blokes—went off and talked about the future of the law centre movement. I thought this was daft: everyone should be involved in these discussions. But I think the white blokes genuinely thought they were treating everyone equally.

John, Colin and I felt that just because the service we offered was free it didn't mean it had to be shabby. We felt that the people who came through the doors were entitled to the best service possible and to be made to feel welcome. So we smartened up our part of the premises, but none of the staff at the advice centre were interested in doing anything to brighten up their area.

When you are spending each day trying to sort out other people's problems, it's important that you are able to switch off after work. I found that reading helped me unwind. Since completing my O levels I had rediscovered reading. One of the books that influenced me was *The L-Shaped Room* by Lynn Reid Banks, which told the story of the struggles of a young woman who is pregnant and unmarried, and has been thrown out of her father's home. I also read *Our Flag Stays Red* by Phil Piratin, the first Communist councillor in London and later an MP. I watched a short video called *The Life and Times of Rosie the Riveter*, about women working in munitions factory in America during the Second World War, and thought it was incredibly powerful.

I also liked to get out of London and spend some time in the countryside. In 1981 I went as a helper with some of the kids at Archbishop Michael Ramsey School when they went camping to Devon. This was the year that Prince Charles married Diana Spencer; so we staged our own royal wedding. Jeffrey played Charles and a black pupil played the Archbishop of Canterbury. The kids thought it was brilliant.

That same year, I began a legal executive course at a college on Gray's Inn Road. I never looked forward to going there each Tuesday. I found it boring. But I went because, if Southwark Council withdrew the Law Centre's funding, which was always likely, I knew I would stand more chance of getting another job.

By now I had become good friends with Harriet Harman. When a by-election was declared in Peckham in 1982, she decided to stand. She used to drive to my flat in Wyndham Road in her Mini to tidy herself up and have some tea before going out canvassing.

On the night of the election, I went with her to the count at Peckham town hall. I'd helped run polling stations in local elections and attended the count, but it was the first time I'd ever been to a count for a parliamentary constituency. It was Harriet's first time as well. Waiting for the results to be announced was incredibly exciting. Harriet won by a majority of nearly 4,000.

We sometimes went for a drink at a wine bar in Camberwell, where we sat in the corner putting the world to rights. Sometimes she and Jack Dromey would come for Sunday lunch, or I'd visit them. She was pregnant by then, and I remember her telling me how exhausting she found being an MP.

The following year, Bob Mellish resigned as MP for Bermondsey and Simon Hughes was elected. The Labour candidate was Peter Tatchell, who had come out as gay many years before. The reason he wasn't elected was because his face didn't fit, not because of his sexuality. He was seen as a mad leftie—and he was from Australia. But his decision to stand in the by-election led to him being attacked for his sexuality. John O'Grady, the leader of Southwark Council, toured the constituency on the back of a horse and cart, singing a song that referred to Tatchell 'wearing his trousers back to front'. A lot of people thought O'Grady was a disgrace.

I used to attend meetings at the North Southwark Community Development Project, just off Borough High Street. Its main focus was planning, as by the late 1970s property developers had started taking an interest in the abandoned buildings and land along the river in Bermondsey. I remember a young doctor from Guy's Hospital saying at a meeting that the hospital was in danger of losing its status as a teaching hospital because it didn't have enough of a variety of patients. Most of those who went to Guy's were elderly.

One of the North Southwark Community Development Project's largest campaigns was to turn Coin Street, a derelict area along the river near Waterloo Station, into housing at affordable rents for local people. A property developer's attempts to buy the land for offices led to a legal battle. John Hobson represented the local people and won the day. It was a fantastic victory for the power of local people against big companies. John went on to become a barrister specialising in planning law.

I attended several meetings of the London Docklands Development Corporation (LDDC), a quango set up in 1981 to bring life back to London's docklands. It had begun a programme to regenerate the wharves and warehouses that dotted the narrow streets along the river around London Bridge and Tower Bridge. The LDDC's plan was to attract new industries to encourage people to work and live in the area.

I often joked with the staff at the Southwark Law Centre that we were against everything and in favour of nothing. For instance, we campaigned against the building of both the Globe Theatre and City Airport. Our view was that the former docks should be for people, which meant building social housing. Poor old Sam Wannamaker must have thought we were mad. We didn't think that a theatre would be for local people. It would be for outsiders, posh people. We objected to the plans to build City Airport because of the noise.

I found campaigning for changes in the community very exciting. There was a great feeling of anything being possible. We never started our own campaigns, unlike many organizations. All our campaigns were based on what local people wanted.

Everyone at the Law Project joined the Transport and General Workers' union (T&G). We were known as the

1/208 branch, representing voluntary groups in Southwark. Colin gave everyone in the branch a task. Mine was to provide information about training courses. I was elected as the branch representative to the general management committee of the Peckham Labour Party.

In the summer of 1981, I went to the T&G's week-long annual summer school held at the Royal Agricultural College in Cirencester. Around 100 members from across the country and from Ireland took part. This was my first experience of the union as a national organization.

Each day, I attended talks and discussion groups. I learnt about the formation of the T&G in 1922 when the Dockers' Union and the Transport Workers' Federation amalgamated. I was fascinated to learn about Ernest Bevin, the T&G's first general secretary, a visionary figure who had been an official in the Dockers' Union and who led the T&G in support of the miners in the General Strike of 1926. Among other things, Bevin called for a state pension at sixty, invalidity benefits for those wounded in the war, raising the school leaving age to sixteen, and a forty-five-hour working week.

The summer school took place against the backdrop of the troubles in Northern Ireland. The majority of the workers in Northern Ireland were Protestant, and there was a long history of the T&G supporting Protestants. But the leadership and members in the 1970s and 1980s recognized that it should support the workers, whatever their faith. What impressed me greatly was how they were able to steer a course between the two sides. This was achieved by not looking at a person as either a Catholic or a Protestant but as an individual. Religion didn't matter in the T&G. We had Catholic and Protestant members who worked closely together, babysitting each other's kids and helping each other out.

I was surprised to find that I was one of only four women attending the school. When I raised this in a meeting, everyone there just nodded, but didn't seem that concerned. But I found it pretty odd.

In March I attended my first TUC Women's Conference in Scarborough. Its aim was to promote greater involvement by women in the trade-union movement. We had met at Transport House in November to discuss the motions and the agenda, but we had no say in these as they had already been put forward by Marie Patterson, the T&G women's officer, so I thought it was all a bit pointless.

I was asked to represent the Association of Clerical, Technical and Supervisory Staff, the T&G's white-collar group, on the London and south-east women's regional advisory committee. In 1981 the union had accepted a resolution that there should be women's advisory committees for each region. Because the computer system at the office for the London region didn't distinguish between men and women, the union didn't even know how many female members it had. Every trade group had a representative. The woman who represented the lorry drivers was actually a secretary—people nicknamed her Yorkie after the TV chocolate advert.

Although the committee was supposed to represent women, it was chaired by a man, who had worked at Goodyear Tyres. At the first meeting, at the regional office in Green Lanes in north London, he said, 'Now come on, girls, I know how you like to talk. But we have to be orderly here, so only one person will talk at a time.' I was gobsmacked by this. At the Law Centre I was treated as an equal, but he seemed to think we were all stupid. We ended up calling him Daffy Duck, because he was an idiot.

But the beginnings of these women's advisory committees were not easy. Members were not allowed to attend regional committee meetings, where decisions were made, so the issues they discussed never went anywhere. For example, at that time in order to become a bus inspector on the London buses you had to be a bus driver first. The union on the buses was very well organized. But you could only be a driver if you were a certain height because of the way the cab was designed. We raised this issue on our committee and said we would like to discuss it with the bus committee and look at how this rule could be changed. The bus committee told us this was none of our business, as it was an industrial matter. This was an example of indirect sexual discrimination.

On another occasion the T&G had refused to take up the case of a group of part-time women workers in a factory in the Midlands. When redundancies had been announced, the union had agreed with the employer that all the part-time workers should go first. Most of the part-time workers were women and many had worked at the factory for much longer than the men. When the women asked the local union to take up their case on the grounds of sex discrimination, it refused. They then asked Marie Patterson, the national women's officer, to support them. She also refused. Moss Evans, the general secretary, didn't think the union needed to be involved. In my opinion, this was a black mark for the union, as this was a ground-breaking case about women's rights at work. In the end, Harriet Harman, who was then an officer at the National Council for Civil Liberties, took on the case and the women won.

This kind of attitude to women was deeply entrenched in the T&G. I received a letter from a woman who worked part-time in the office of a coach-building company, and who had been told by her union officer that she wasn't allowed to join the union. I thought this was outrageous and wrote a stiff letter to him. He wrote back telling me to mind my own business.

I was not going to mind my own business. Quite the reverse. It was my business. I was going to do something to make sure women were given the same voice as men in the union.

6. You'll Do

IN THE 1980S, the T&G was one of the country's largest and most powerful unions. It was split into eleven regions, each with a regional secretary and regional organizer. In February 1983 the Southwark Law Project seconded me to the T&G office at Southall in west London. When Jack Dromey was appointed national public services officer, he had recommended that I cover his former job of district organizer in Southall until a full-time appointment was made. Unlike some unions, the T&G had a policy of only appointing union members to paid posts. I was thrilled at the prospect of getting involved in a union, even though it would take me two hours to get to work from my home in Camberwell.

As a local organizer (although I was known as a 'stand down officer' because I was only temporary), I was the most junior union official. Unlike regional organizers, local organizers didn't cover geographical areas, but one of the fourteen trade groups who made up the T&G. These included road transport, public transport, vehicle-building, the docks, construction and textiles.

I would be responsible for the power and engineering workers employed at local factories such as Thorn EMI and Gillette. My role would be to represent them when they had grievances and negotiate pay and conditions with the management. Although I had experience negotiating with housing and benefits officers, I didn't have any experience negotiating pay; but I've always believed that things should be right and fair, backed up by solid evidence, and that if you are reasonable, and listen to the other point of view, then you can usually find a meeting place in the middle.

I hadn't been to Southall before, although I knew that it had one of the largest Asian populations in the country.

Walking down the high street, smelling the spices from the Indian restaurants and gazing at the colourful saris in the shop windows, it felt a world away from Walworth Road.

The T&G premises were just off the high street. I shared a small office upstairs with two women who spent the day clattering away on typewriters or pouring over bulging grey Lever Arch files. I thought it was quite telling that the women were still using manual typewriters. When I worked in the accounts office of Holland, Hannen and Cubitts back in 1958 we had all used electronic typewriters. Yet the T&G officers, who were all men, had a new car every year. If the union could afford new cars for the men, why couldn't it give women modern typewriters?

Another thing that struck me was that there were no Asian workers employed in the office. I mentioned this to an official one day.

'They don't apply,' he said abruptly.

I understood by this that he was saying I should mind my own business. I didn't mention the matter again, but it did make me start to wonder how representative the union really was. I found myself thinking about this again and it fired me up. I felt something wasn't quite right. Wasn't the T&G supposed to be about equality?

I felt I had to prove myself in the job, both because I was a woman and because I was new. At the same time, I knew some in the union would only ever see me in terms of my sex, not my ability.

The first meeting with management I had was to negotiate the annual pay round for the workers who operated the fuel pumps for the planes at Heathrow. Although they only worked in a small area of the airport, they were very powerful. If they ever decided to come out on strike, Heathrow would grind to a halt. I don't remember much about the meeting other than thinking how smart all the managers sitting around the table looked. As I left, I told myself that I needed to buy myself a new suit.

I could tell that when I met the management in some companies they were surprised that a woman should turn up. Despite this, I never felt they didn't take me seriously. The workers didn't mind that I was a woman, so long as they could see that I knew what I was doing. I once went to a meeting at an engineering factory that operated a very complicated payment by results scheme. An official from the electrical union was supposed to attend but he never turned up. When I told the shop stewards that I was finding it difficult to understand the scheme, they sat down with me and patiently explained how it all worked.

Some nights I used to work late in the office. When an elderly official realized that I was often alone in the building, he told me he was going to speak to Sid Staden, the regional secretary for London and the south-east.

'Blimey! Don't do that,' I said. The last thing I wanted was for the regional secretary to think that I expected different treatment. I never would have been taken seriously again.

'Well, you shouldn't be here alone late at night.'

'I'm not anxious. I'm more worried for my safety in Camberwell, where I live, than I am here.'

He didn't seem convinced and went away muttering to himself.

In June 1983 when the vacancy for a district organizer, based at the union office in Camberwell, came up I decided to apply for it. The union employed around 420 officers in mainland Britain, Northern Ireland and the Republic of Ireland. As I'd been doing the same job in Southall for a few months, I figured I might stand a chance of getting it. I remembered the words of my mum: you're no better or no worse than anyone else. On the other hand, I knew that there was favouritism in the union, that people often got jobs because so–and-so felt they could work well with them. This meant that you could be brilliant but not get a job, or useless and get a job.

I was delighted when I was told that I had an interview. To prepare for it I went round to see Jack Dromey, who lived with Harriet Harman a few streets away. Queen Victoria once said of Gladstone that he spoke to her as if she was a public meeting. You could say the same about Jack. I sat down with him in the living room and he produced leaflets and publicity material. At local level, you rarely got to see this kind of information. It was usually only senior officials who got to see it. He also showed me copies of agreements for manual workers in local government and ancillary staff in the NHS.

Jack let me take the pile of papers home with me. I took two days off work and sat at the kitchen table reading through all the documents and making notes on an A4 pad. Some of the information was incredibly complicated and I knew I wouldn't be able to remember it.

The interview took place at the regional office in north London. I don't remember much about it except that one of the officials on the panel asked me, 'What is the agreement for ancillary staff in the NHS?' Thanks to Jack, I knew my stuff.

The next day I received a phone call to say that I had got the job. I was over the moon, not just because of the job but also because I wouldn't have to make that long journey to Southall each day. The office was just a few minutes' walk from my flat.

But now I was going to be a permanent union official it meant that I had to say goodbye to everyone at the Southwark Law Project. I had thoroughly enjoyed my time there and I had learnt a huge amount. I would also miss the camaraderie and the lively discussions about politics we'd had.

Before taking up my new job, I went on holiday with some friends to Brittany in France. My mum was ill at this time, but I knew my sisters would visit her while I was away. We rented a house in a small village and had a wonderful time. It was just the kind of rest I needed. When I returned, I was told by one of my sisters that Mum had died. She had been admitted to St Mary's Hospital in Paddington after developing breast cancer, which then spread to her brain. It emerged that she had found a lump in December but hadn't told anyone because she didn't want to spoil our Christmas. I was devastated and wished I had been at her bedside and that I had been able to support my sisters. We had always been a close family and had always been there for each other. My mum's death didn't really hit me until a few weeks after the funeral. When I realised that she was gone forever I felt like an orphan. I wanted her back so much.

With these feelings swirling around inside me, focusing on my new job was not easy. My role was to work with the public sector workers in local government and the NHS. These included manual ancillary staff at Lambeth, Richmond and Merton councils and at the Epsom cluster of hospitals for the mentally ill. Over the years, there had been a series of different union officers dealing with the hospital staff. Sid Staden didn't consider those doing manual jobs in hospitals to be on the same level as the dockers. Because of all this, it wasn't surprising that many ancillary workers had mixed feelings about the T&G.

What's more, the Thatcher government had introduced compulsory competitive tendering, which opened up many services to private competition, leaving public sector workers fearing for their jobs and wages.

As a district organizer, I had to become familiar with all the rules and regulations governing relations between unions and employers. This wasn't easy. In those days, manual workers in local government came under the buff book and white-collar workers came under the purple book. These books, which ran to hundreds of pages, covered agreements between the unions and the employers. They were referred to by senior shop stewards and were full of minute details about every aspect of the working day.

Being a district organizer also meant I had to resign from the London and South-East region women's advisory committee, as it was only for lay members. Nevertheless, I resolved to stay in touch with the members.

Not long after I had started in the job, Maurice Smith, the branch secretary of the Epsom hospitals, came over to meet me one day. Small, fat and scruffy with long hair, he was known by everyone as 'Mad Maurice'. When he walked into the office he stood there, looking me up and down, and eventually said, 'Mm. You'll do.'

I was taken aback. 'Oh, thanks very much,' I said, trying not to sound too sarcastic.

And when I was introduced to the branch secretary at Lambeth Council, the first thing he said to me was, 'And what does a woman know about the "Lambeth dust"?'

'Enough. And I'm sure I'll learn lots more about them when I meet them,' I said.

He gave a snort and walked out.

It wasn't just the dustmen in Lambeth Council who clashed with management. Disputes were common with other groups of workers. On Christmas Eve I received a phone call from the branch secretary for social services. Relations between the drivers of the Lambeth ambulances and management were strained. At one time, the drivers would take a group of elderly people to a day centre, or take some children with special needs to a centre, and then sit around all day doing nothing until it was time to collect them in the afternoon. Needless to say, the management's decision to give the drivers other jobs while they were waiting had proved very unpopular.

'We're on the stones,' said the branch secretary, meaning they had gone out on strike. He explained that the previous night a driver had been stopped by the police, breathalysed and found to be over the limit.

'He'd been driving elderly people to Christmas parties and then collecting them,' he said.

'So why was he breathalysed?' I asked.

'He'd had a couple of drinks at the day centres. That was all.'

The branch secretary felt this was a justification for the driver's drinking, so he had called the members out on strike. I knew I had to try and persuade them to return to work, so I immediately set off for the Lambeth depot on Stockwell Road.

When I arrived, I found all the drivers sitting in a Portakabin, smoking and playing cards.

'Nothing is going to happen today,' I said.

'What do you mean?' said a wiry man.

'It's Christmas Eve. We'll have to wait until after the Christmas holiday so we can have a discussion with the management.'

'That's no good. We want a meeting now,' insisted the branch secretary.

I phoned the manager and we agreed to stick to our guns and tell the men that there would be no meeting till after Christmas. I guessed that way they would all be less wound up when the meeting eventually took place. They were not happy but could see that was how things were. Besides because it was Christmas Eve they wanted to get off and go home or down to the pub.

Soon after this, when three road workers were sacked by Lambeth after one of the bosses caught them laying tarmac on the drive of a house, I represented them at a disciplinary hearing at Lambeth town hall.

'I think you need to look at the situation in a sympathetic way,' I said, pointing out that the asphalt the men used was waste. So if they hadn't used it the council would have had to pay to dispose of it. This was the only thing I could think of to try and defend the three men, but I had to work hard to keep a straight face.

'I don't accept that,' said the personnel officer, looking at me as if I was mad. 'They shouldn't have done what they did.'

Despite my plea for leniency, the three men were dismissed. I left the hearing feeling disappointed that I had let them down. I felt sorry for them. What they did was wrong, but with all the cuts taking pace in local authorities they were going to find it difficult to get another job.

I also represented a young man who worked in the kitchen at Kingston Hospital. He was always late. Somehow I managed to persuade the management to give him one more chance. After the hearing, I said to him, 'If you're late again, you're on your own. Who do you think gets on with the work in the kitchen while you are still in bed?'

'Dunno,' he murmured.

'It's your mates who are lugging saucepans around and cleaning the ovens. Is that fair?'

He seemed quite shocked by my attitude. He didn't seem to understand how his laziness affected the other workers who made sure they were punctual.

Back then, because the Health and Safety at Work Act didn't apply to hospitals, health and safety inspectors were not allowed to visit. This led to some very lax procedures, especially in kitchens, which are always chaotic and volatile places. When I went to a hospital in Epsom to meet the kitchen staff, I was horrified to find a man standing on a ladder fixing a light, while on the counter underneath him was a large tray of chips, completely uncovered.

One interesting thing I learnt as a district organizer was that it was common to find workers of a particular nationality doing the same job. For example, many of those working as porters or cleaners in the hospitals in Epsom were Spanish, while many school cleaners in South London were Portuguese. This said a lot about word-of-mouth recruitment, which was known to be unfair and exclusive.

As I mentioned earlier, many local authorities were implementing compulsory competitive tendering to provide services. The argument for it was that it would cut costs and improve value for money. In reality, it meant that some low-paid workers lost their jobs and others had their wages reduced. I had to meet with school dinner-ladies, kitchen staff and cleaners in Richmond, where the council had decided to introduce what they called 'cook and chill'. Instead of school meals being cooked on site, they would now be cooked off site and heated up in the school kitchens. I had to explain to the women what was happening and that they would be paid less. Quite rightly they were angry and wanted to know why the union wasn't doing more to help them. I didn't know what to say to them. I too felt that the union should be doing much more. But I knew that because compulsory competitive tendering affected mainly women, it wasn't prioritized by the T&G leadership.

In 1984 when I heard that there was going to be a vacancy for the national women's officer, based at Transport House, the T&G's central office in Smith Square, Westminster, I decided to apply for it. It seemed like a job made for me. The vacancy had arisen after Marie Patterson resigned. She had been in the job for many years and said that she had had enough and wanted to return to her kitchen. When I heard this, I thought this sounded an odd thing to say. Later, it was alleged that her husband, a journalist, had given a solicitor credentials so he could attend the TUC Congress to serve legal papers on Arthur Scargill during the miners' strike that had started earlier in the year.

That month, I attended my first Labour Party conference, in Blackpool, representing my constituency in Peckham. The conference was buzzing with talk about the miners' strike, which exposed the divisions between the Militant Tendency and those backing Neil Kinnock's attempts to reform the party. Neil Kinnock was sponsored by the T&G, and before being elected an MP he had been a tutor at T&G summer schools. He always had a lot to say for himself.

During the break at the morning session, I got chatting over a cup of tea to Walter Greendale, the chair of the T&G general executive council and a former docker.

'Do you think I should apply for the national women's officer job?' I asked him.

'Well, there will be a few people after it, you know,' he said.

'Do you reckon?'

'Mind you, I suppose it will have to go to a woman because of the seat on the TUC general council.'

The TUC had reserved six seats on its general council for women. Walter was telling me that if it wasn't for this, then the union would appoint a man to the job of women's officer. I thought this was hilarious. What a farce.

One evening in the bar at the hotel I was staying at I wandered up to Moss Evans. A small, round man, he was originally from South Wales and had succeeded Jack Jones as general secretary in 1978.

'I think the union could be doing much more for women,' I suggested, hoping that he might listen to what I had to say. I wanted to be sure that a T&G delegate would speak in the equality debate.

'Listen! We've got far more important things to think about,' he snarled.

'But—'

'The union doesn't have time to be bothering with this sort of thing,' he said.

Shocked, I turned and walked away, thinking he seemed a nasty piece of work. I might have felt that there was no point in applying to be national women's officer. With the head of the union so negative about women, what was the point? But I didn't. Moss Evans' attitude made me want the job even more. The T&G had to change, and I was prepared to do everything I could to make this happen.

A few weeks later, on a cold November morning, I left my home in Camberwell and caught the bus to Westminster. I was wearing a dark grey skirt, navy blue woolly tights, red shoes and a red jumper. Entering Transport House I felt both apprehensive and excited. I hadn't made a very good impression on Moss Evans, so maybe he wasn't going to be on my side. And, even though Jack Dromey had given me T&G policy documents and copies of the national agreement between the Confederation of Shipbuilding and Engineering Unions and the Engineering Employers' Federation, I wondered if I would be able to answer all the questions about union procedures and policies. I knew I would be facing some tough ones. But I reminded myself that I had the ability and enthusiasm to do the job well. I was passionate about fighting for a better deal for working women.

The interview was held in the finance and general purposes meeting room. On the wall were paintings and photos of all the general secretaries, from Ernest Bevin to Jack Jones. Sitting around a mahogany horseshoe-shaped table were a glum-looking Moss Evans, Alex Kitson, the deputy general secretary and eleven members of the finance and general purposes committee, a sub-committee of the executive. Not for the first time, I was the only woman in the room. Ray Collins, the central office manager, whom I had met when I attended meetings of the TUC women's conference, was also there, to take notes. This lifted my spirits a little, as he believed the union should be doing much more for women.

When I took my seat, Moss Evans smiled thinly at me and said, 'Explain to us the union's position on defence.'

Defence was a tricky area for the unions. On the one hand, we were against using military power but, on the other hand, thousands of members were employed in the armaments and aircraft industries.

'Well, it's a complicated one, as many union members are employees in companies manufacturing weapons,' I said, and then talked about the policy of developing alternative employment opportunities.

I caught the London region representative, a former docker, winking at me across the table. I thought to myself, either he thinks I'm doing okay, or he's going to do me in. But I couldn't work out which.

Towards the end of the interview, Alex Kitson said, 'Tell us how many sponsored MPs the union has.'

I couldn't think of the answer. I thought this was a very peculiar question. 'I'm really sorry but I can't answer that.' Then I quickly added, 'I do know that the list covers one page in the union diary.' As soon as I had said this, I realized how ridiculous it sounded.

'Okay. Can you tell us, then, how many sponsored MPs there are in your region?'

I was so flustered that I couldn't answer that question either. 'Er, no. I'm sorry.'

As I left the interview, I began mentally to list all the sponsored MPs, but it was too late. When I got home, I couldn't make my mind up if I had done well or not. Then it struck me that I hadn't been asked a single question about women in the union and what I might do to get them more involved.

At about 9.00 p.m. Jack Dromey phoned. 'Margaret, I've got some news,' he said excitedly.

'Go on,' I said. 'Tell me that they've decided to give it to someone else.'

'You've got the job!'

He explained that he had spoken to Bill Morris, the national officer for the passenger transport trade group, and that Morris had told him that the Midlands region representative at the interview had said the panel had agreed to offer me the job.

I dropped the phone and ran into the living room, where Jeffrey, Carol and Stella were sprawled on the settee watching TV.

'Guess what? I've got the job!'

The three of them leapt up and threw their arms around me and we all danced about. I felt relieved that I would be leaving the job of district organizer in Camberwell, as I had found some of the members very difficult to work with.

Marie Patterson was due to leave the job just before Christmas and I would begin in the first week of January. In the preceding weeks Marie took me to meet some of the management and senior stewards at a number of factories and offices. On one occasion we were on a train going to Birmingham when she said, 'Whenever you travel away from London, take a extra skirt with you.'

'Oh, why?'

'Because you never know when your zip might break.'

I thought to myself: well if this is the most profound advice you can give, then it's not worth much.

I went with her to a Christmas party a few weeks later at the head office of ASLEF, the train drivers' union, which was in a house in Hampstead. It was a very jolly evening and a lot of people had too much to drink. I left the party with Ada Maddocks, the women's officer for NALGO and a member of the TUC general council. As she was sozzled, I gripped her arm to help down the steps from the house. It wasn't easy, as Ada was quite large and I'm quite small and petite. It was very dark and she missed a step and went flying into some bushes. It took all my strength to help her up. Eventually, with her swaying from side to side, I guided her into the street, where I flagged down a cab, heaved her into the back and told the driver to take her home to Essex.

I knew the major issue I would face in the job was that, apart from Ray Collins, no one at the top in the union seemed to care about the rights of women workers, who now made up about half the workforce. The leadership didn't think there was any difference between male and female workers. They thought that treating everyone the same was all that was required. But women workers were disadvantaged in so many ways. They had to look after children and they hadn't been given the kind of training opportunities men had. Also many women were employed part-time, which meant they didn't have the same kind of employment protection as full-time workers. But I didn't really know at this stage what the issues were on which women would follow me. Nor could I guess the struggles I would have to convince officials that women were being treated as second-class citizens by the union.

7. It's a Man's World

OFFICIALLY THE TITLE of my new post was 'national woman officer', but I decided to call myself national women's officer. As far as I was concerned, my job was to look after women. At this time, out of the 400 paid organizers in the T&G, only four were women. Yet most of the 200 or so staff employed at Transport House were women.

My remit was to do any work required by the general executive council and Moss Evans, the general secretary. My brief also included responsibility for white-collar engineering workers at companies such as GEC and Thorn EMI. If issues couldn't be resolved at local level, then I would be brought in to negotiate. I realized, however, that with no clear job description I would have to make up the job as I went along. This suited me fine.

With around three million on the dole, the mid-1980s were a turbulent and uncertain period for the T&G. Once it had been a force to be reckoned with in British politics, but now, as a result of huge job losses in industries such as car manufacturing and engineering, its membership was declining and at the same its political influence. The Thatcher government had set about stifling the power of the unions by introducing a raft of anti-union laws, including outlawing mass picketing and closed-shop ballots. If workers wanted to take industrial action, they now had to hold a secret ballot with all sorts of complicated rules about timing and the notice that had to be given to the employer. Legislation had also been passed giving employers the right to sue unions. The sale of council houses created a class of people who saw themselves as aspirational, which was a good thing. But they didn't see the unions as speaking up for them any more. This was all made more difficult by the fact that the Labour Party was in disarray and seemed to be run by the hard left.

If all this wasn't bad enough, the T&G was embroiled in a bitter power struggle at the top, where a split had opened up between those on the broad left and those on the right. Myself, Moss Evans, Ron Todd, Bill Morris and Walter Greendale were on the left, while most of the regional secretaries were on the right. Two of the most influential were George Wright, the regional secretary for Wales, and Albert Blyghton, the legal secretary and someone with a reputation as a fixer.

Generally speaking, those on the right saw the trade-union movement simply as a body that looked after its members, while those on the left saw it also as a vehicle for political change. In most cases, those on the right were the more qualified members—electricians, plumbers, engineers and civil servants. The secretaries of these groups weren't interested in campaigning on issues that didn't directly affect their membership.

The regional secretaries were some of the most powerful figures in the T&G, controlling their own budgets and setting their own agenda. They didn't like central office interfering. Many were also known for their strong views.

I had only been in my new post a few days when Sid Staden popped his head around the door of my office to ask how I was getting on.

'I'm doing fine, Sid,' I said.

'Margaret, we treat everyone equal. We don't need to do anything special for women,' he said, sitting down.

'But, Sid, you can't treat everyone equally if some people are not starting on an equal footing.' He couldn't see that women had been treated as second-class citizens in the union for years.

'What about these feminists?'

'What do you mean?' I knew he was talking about the women's advisory committee members.

'Well, do all of these kind of women hate men?'

'Actually I don't think any of them do, Sid. A lot of them are happily married.'

Theoretically Sid understood the arguments about women's rights, but in practice he couldn't seem to get his head around them. Like most senior officials, he couldn't understand how they related to the day-to-day activities of the union, where men had always run things. This had been the way of thinking in the T&G since it was formed.

When a motion was put forward at the annual conference in 1947 for more women officers in the union, the general secretary, Arthur Deakin, dismissed it, saying that women had the same opportunities as men and would receive precisely the same consideration as men when applying for posts. It was, of course, nonsense. In fact, forty years on, the union still had only four women officers.

When I was younger, if a woman wanted to take out a hire-purchase agreement she could only do it with the permission of her husband. A woman's place was supposed to be in the home and she was expected to be subservient to her husband. It wasn't until the 1970s that legislation was introduced to give women the same rights as men. The Equal Pay Act came into force in 1975 and the Sex Discrimination Act was passed the same year.

In 1984 the European court decided that the UK's equal pay legislation wasn't strong enough and the government had to amend it. One of the first cases brought under the new law was that of a woman employed as a cook in a shipyard in the north-west. She argued that her job had the same value as that of a welder. She won.

But none of this legislation seemed to have made much impact on how the T&G was run. If I was going to persuade men such as Sid that the union had to change the way it viewed women members, I knew I would have to be rational, flexible and patient. I'd seen some women in the trade-union movement go over the top and get nowhere. Furthermore,

I would only be respected and have any influence if I was seen to be doing my job as well as any man.

I had to make sure that no one thought of me as some kind of raving feminist. I had never been drawn to the kind of radical feminist movement that emerged in the 1960s. I never read *Spare Rib* magazine or wanted to get involved in the protests over nuclear weapons at Greenham Common. I was too busy looking after Joe and feeding my kids to think about burning my bra. These sorts of women were middle-class and didn't share the concerns I had about working women. I have to admit, though, that they paved the way for the changes that eventually took place.

But their confrontational approach wouldn't have worked with the T&G. I've always believed that you will never get anything from a person if you shout and bawl at them. You have to be respectful, no matter how much you disagree with someone's viewpoint, and win them over through rational arguments. I believed I had to show that the changes I wanted would make life better for the regional secretaries. They would bring added value. Anyway, it was no good falling out with them, as they were far more powerful than me.

I faced two big problems with the regional secretaries. One was that I was promoting something that many of them didn't believe was important, and the other was that I was on the left. One of the first things I did was to draw up a list of senior officers around the country who were likely to be sympathetic to women's issues. Out of the eleven regional secretaries I identified only three. So I decided to focus on working with them and ignore the others. I needed to show that the work we were doing was going to be helpful to them. Somebody once said to me, 'Never question anyone's motives; they will always be bad.' I wasn't concerned about their motives. I just wanted to bring about change.

I knew there were a few others in the T&G whom I could count on for support. Among them were Jack Dromey, Bill

Morris and Ray Collins, the general office manager. Ray seemed to know everyone in the T&G and advised me about whom to talk to—and whom not to talk to. Someone else who was a great help in this period was Ann Gibson, secretary of the TUC women's committee.

One of the first meetings I attended in my new post was the national women's advisory committee, which had only recently been set up and had only met once. The aim of the advisory committee was to provide women with a forum for discussion and the exchange of views and experiences. However, the name said a lot. The committee was advisory; it wasn't part of the main T&G structure. Therefore it didn't have any power to influence policy in the union; you can take advice or leave it.

The meeting was held in the boardroom on the top floor of Transport House. The fact that there wasn't a ladies' loo on the floor, only a gents', spoke volumes. The committee was made up of representatives from each of the regional women's advisory committees. I had met most of them at the TUC Congress or at the TUC women's conference. Everyone told me that they were so happy that they now had a women's officer they could talk to. Marie Patterson hadn't been very approachable.

Jane McKay, who was employed by the Scottish TUC, chaired the meeting. She was a member of the Communist Party and had been very active in CND and the Chile Solidarity Campaign. I was the secretary. After I had welcomed everyone and dealt with items on the agenda from the previous meeting and explained what would be happening at the TUC women's conference in Scarborough in March, I opened up the floor. It wasn't long before simmering resentment boiled over.

'The union doesn't seem to think it matters that there aren't many women on the committees,' said Val, a shop steward at a pharmaceutical company in Hull.

'It's women who do most of the part-time jobs. But you can't join a pension scheme if you are employed part-time,' said Margaret, the shop steward at Cadbury's in Dublin.

Listening to these women express their views, and their anger, lifted my spirits and made me feel that things could and would change in the union.

If the work of the women's committee was going to be effective, then we needed to form close relationships with each other and make sure we were all informed on developments in the union. So I insisted that we had a lunch break during the committee meetings. I felt this was very important. Most of the other committees worked through lunch. So we all went to a nearby café, where we could chat and get to know each other. This simple change worked wonders. We all became friends and would often phone each other at home to discuss issues that concerned us.

Part of my job involved explaining the work of the women's advisory committee to the other T&G committees. In order to get on to any of the committees in the T&G, you really had to know your stuff. When I asked the chair of the food and drink committee where one of the members worked and he said he didn't know, I was astonished.

'What do you mean you don't know?'

'I don't know where he works,' he shrugged.

I was stunned by his answer, as I knew every member of the women's advisory committee.

'Well, I can tell you where every one of the women on my committee works. I can tell you if they are married or not, if they have children, and what the husband is like.'

He didn't know what to say. I think my reply had floored him.

I was sitting in my office one morning opening the post when one letter stopped me in my tracks. It was from Peter Bottomley, the minister for employment, inviting me to meet him at his office to talk about my work. The Thatcher government appeared to be hell-bent on destroying the trade unions, so why was Bottomley interested in meeting me? When I told one of my colleagues about this, he explained that Bottomley had been president of the Conservative Trade Unionists. I didn't even know there were Conservative trade unionists. So I went to meet him and he was perfectly charming. I can't remember what we talked about, but what I do remember is sitting there feeling a nervous wreck, as I didn't really know what I was going to do in my new job.

My first speech as national women's officer was in front of a large audience of union members at Manchester town hall. I recall looking out from the podium and seeing a sea of male faces.

I have always been someone who takes a practical approach to everything in life and likes to get stuck in. Action always speaks louder then words. I knew that if I really wanted to understand how the union could support its women members better then I had to get out of the office and talk to them at work. So I began by visiting some of the places where the women on the advisory committee worked. For example, I went to Reckitt's pharmaceutical factory in Hull, a Coca-Cola bottling plant near Manchester and a hospital.

Most weeks I did my best to visit a factory or other workplace. One of the worst places I visited was a factory near Rotherham in South Yorkshire, where they made chunky glass ashtrays for pubs. The heat and noise from the furnace were awful. I had never been anywhere so hot or noisy.

When I walked around the assembly lines of the Ford plant in Dagenham, the only female worker I saw was the nurse. It had been the Ford sewing-machinists, making seat covers, who had been instrumental in getting Barbara Castle, the secretary of state for employment in the Wilson government, to introduce the Equal Pay Act of 1970. The women had gone on strike because they felt they should be paid the same as the male workers who cut the cloth.

One thing I discovered was that food factories were awful places to work. They were either hot and smelly or freezing cold with condensation dripping from the ceiling. At a factory in Peterborough where small containers of fruit salad were produced, lines of women wearing white overalls stood at steel sinks, peeling apples, plums, melons and other fruit under running water. At Premier Brands in the north-west, I watched women leaning over making Swiss rolls, and thought to myself that they were all going to end up with bad backs.

Some of the women I met on the shop floor were inspiring. One of the most impressive was Doris Fernandes, a shop steward in a bottling plant in Lancashire. She introduced a rotation scheme so that the workers did a variety of jobs and she also persuaded the management to allow women to drive forklift trucks and to provide part-time workers with pensions. This was radical stuff.

Wandering around these factories was fascinating. I nearly always came away having learnt some titbit of information. For instance, I discovered that the mills in Lancashire produced cotton, whereas the mills in Yorkshire produced wool. At Cadbury's in Birmingham I was informed that there was only one person who made chocolate buttons. A single machine did all the work.

While relations between workers and management were, on the whole, quite good in the private sector, it was a different story with some of our members in the public sector, where, all too often, there was an attitude of 'we do what we are paid to do and we're not going to do any more'. I've always believed that there has to be give and take in life.

The autumn of 1985 was a hectic time for me. Carol and Jeffrey, who, coincidentally, were both working in nurseries in Lewisham, got married within a few weeks of each other. I had now passed my driving test and, as I was an official, the T&G had given me a car, a beige Ford Sierra 1400. It was really too big for me as a new driver. I would have much preferred a Mini.

The T&G also provided me with a mortgage, and I bought a semi-detached house in Thornton Heath. The street seemed quiet and pleasant when I first saw it. However, I hadn't been living there long when I started getting problems with the neighbours next door. Most nights there was either loud music blaring, shouting or fights. When I spoke to one of them, he was very apologetic, but he seemed to be spaced out. The noise was driving me nuts. My new job was pressurized and I was working long hours. All I wanted to do when I got home was relax and get a good night's sleep. I complained to a local councillor and he promised to sort out the problem. But he didn't do anything and the noise continued. So eventually I found out where the landlord lived and went to see him. Soon after, he sold the house and a nice couple moved in.

Ron Todd, a former shop steward at Ford in Dagenham, had now succeeded Moss Evans as general secretary. Moss retired early because of ill health. Ron and I had first met when I was a district organizer. A fast talker, he was always very friendly and smoked like a chimney. He loved to tell jokes and he remembered everyone's name. Later, when he became chairman of the TUC's international committee and travelled a lot, he amazed everyone by always remembering the names of every union representative and foreign official he had met.

Ron was far more outward-looking than Moss Evans, and he recognized that the T&G needed to change, because working practices were changing. Yet, while he was against inequality, like Sid Staden he was also unable to make the leap from theory to practice. But it was because of Ron's determination that Bill Morris was elected deputy general secretary, making him the first black senior union official in Britain. Some of the executive general council tried to block Bill because of his colour. But Ron wasn't having it. He was convinced that Bill was the best person for the job.

Bill was born in Jamaica and had emigrated to England in 1954. A former shop steward in Birmingham, he had worked his way up in the T&G, becoming a district organizer in Nottingham, then a district secretary in Northampton and then a national organizer for the passenger services group—in other words, bus drivers, conductors and garage staff.

I had first met him when he was running a campaign against the privatization of the buses and came to the national women's advisory committee to talk about it. He pointed out that the vast majority of those who used buses were women, and if there weren't enough buses running, it would be women who would be affected most. I was so impressed by him. He was the first trade-union official I had heard make the link between the industrial agenda and the community agenda. I had been disappointed that no one in the union seemed to understand this. To me, it was a matter of common sense. So many of the union figures I'd met were too inward-looking, something that has often weakened their position. Furthermore, most had no experience of working outside their own industry. Bill could see that it was vital to let people know how privatizing the buses would affect them, so that they would support the workers.

When Bill took up his post as deputy general secretary in June 1986, I felt that there was now a better chance of getting women's issues to the top of the agenda. Soon after, he came with Ron to the national women's advisory committee. It was clear from the smiles on their faces when they sat down that neither of them expected such a rough ride.

'We're sick to death of being ignored,' said a woman from somewhere in the north.

Ron didn't seem to know what to say. He sat there looking like a rabbit caught in a car's headlights. But Bill nodded, looking genuinely concerned. 'I see,' he said.

'No one takes any notice of what we say,' said someone else. 'You say you're going to do this or that, but nothing ever happens.'

Caroline, who worked in a hospital in the Midlands, thumped the table, sending a glass bouncing into the air. 'We're fed up with it!'

Ron began visibly shaking. He had dealt with dockers and car workers shouting and screaming, but he didn't seem to be able to handle women confronting him. Unlike Bill, Ron couldn't understand that inequality was structural.

In the corridor afterwards Bill turned to me and said, 'You've got a really good bunch of women there.'

'I bloody well have. They are clever and work hard. That's why they are so fed up.'

He grinned and said. 'Margaret, we're going to work well together. But we have a lot to do if we are to bring the T&G into the twentieth century.'

Shortly after, Bill and I met to identify how we might begin to involve women more in the T&G. He agreed with me that the union rules should be changed to allow representatives from each women's advisory committee to attend the regional meetings. These met every three months and were made up of members representing the trades and the districts. But members from the women's committee were not invited to attend, as it was only an advisory committee. We also felt every region should appoint a women's officer and that women-only courses should be set up by every region. We coined a slogan: 'You have to separate to integrate.' In other words, for women to get on the ladder, initiatives had to be introduced just for them.

We produced a questionnaire and sent it to all the regional women's advisory committees to find out how they thought their work could be built into the main work of the union. When we received the replies we presented our findings to Ron. We were delighted when he agreed with our proposals and recommended them to the executive, which accepted the report.

To my amazement, it was also agreed that, as national women's officer, I should attend the executive council. Up until now, only men had sat on the council. I felt I was getting somewhere. But I knew I had to make sure that I didn't get labelled as someone only interested in women's issues.

The T&G has always had an excellent reputation for training and education. In 1982, while still working as an adviser at the Southwark Law Centre, I had attended its first women-only school, or training programme, at the T&G's hotel in Eastbourne, East Sussex. But traditionally far more men than women had benefited from these courses. The centre was equipped with training rooms, a dining room and a bar. The school had been a huge success, and the national women's advisory committee agreed with me that we needed to expand this initiative. Women needed to be better informed about developments in the union and issues that particularly affected them.

So we organized more programmes, which lasted for a week and were designed not just for shop stewards, who were legally entitled to take time off work to attend training, but for any women workers so long as time off could be negotiated with their employer. The programmes covered basic subjects such as how to be a branch secretary; how to deal with grievances and disciplinary matters; how to negotiate; pensions; and the technicalities of equal pay. I thought we needed to offer a broader range of courses, so I met with the education team to discuss this, and we added courses in maternity rights, childcare and part-time working.

I often drove down to the centre to make sure everyone was sorted and things were running smoothly. I used to say to the women, 'You are the foot soldiers out there. You are the ones who have to make other women aware of what's going on.'

Few of the women were well educated in the formal sense, but if you asked them about the agreements they reached with management on issues such as pensions or time and a half, they were red hot on it, even though the issues were often very complex. I told them that just because they had done badly at school, it didn't mean that they weren't intelligent. I encouraged them to believe in themselves more. As time went on, some of the women got into university as mature students and came out with degrees. I was thrilled by this.

Quite often there would be other training courses running at the same time and, of course, these were attended almost exclusively by men. In the bar one Sunday evening a group of dockers began taking mickey out of the women and trying to get off with them. But the women weren't interested.

One of the dockers came over to where I was sitting and said, ''Ere, what's up with them?'

'What do you mean?' I said.

'Not much fun, are they?'

'They are here to learn, not lark around,' I replied. I felt like saying, 'Why would they fancy you?'

For many of the women it hadn't been easy to get to the training course. In many cases, they had to cook a week's dinners for their family and put them in the fridge. At the start of the week, some of the dockers had reacted to the women's lack of interest by arguing with them. But by Thursday night they were all singing and dancing in the bar. When the dockers saw how seriously the women took the training they developed a respect for them. And the women realized that most of the dockers had never worked with women, so they didn't know how to talk to them. I often explained to the male officials on training courses about what we were doing. I did this because, as they were representing women, it was important that they knew about the issues that concerned them.

In March 1985 I was elected to the TUC general council, taking the seat vacated by the previous national women's officer, Marie Patterson. I attended the annual Congress in Blackpool later that year, where I made a speech about the need to improve employment terms and conditions for part-time workers.

When the Tory government had introduced legislation that meant a ballot had to be held before a strike, the unions had opposed it, as it took away their right to control the union rule book. Also, holding a ballot was costly. The government responded by saying that it would pay for the cost of the ballot. The T&G, like most of the unions, was against this. The only union that decided it was going to accept the money was the EETPU (Electrical, Electronic, Telecommunications and Plumbing Union). When the general council met on the Thursday before the conference officially began everyone knew that Eric Hammond, the EETPU general secretary and a right-winger, would defend the union's decision. Eric was a large, well-dressed man. If you met him in your local pub he probably wouldn't have much to say, but you would know he was an authoritative kind of person.

Looking at people such as Rodney Bickerstaff, Norman Willis, Jimmy Knapp and Mick McGahey sitting around me, I felt quite excited to be up with the big boys.

'All the money the EETPU has had been paid by the members. So it doesn't make sense to use this for the ballot when the government is prepared to put the money up,' said Eric.

'It's about principles,' said Ron Todd.

'What do you mean?' asked Eric.

'The money from the government is dirty.'

Eric stood his ground and the meeting became very heated. The general council recommended to the congress that we shouldn't take the money. Because the EETPU refused to abide by this, it was expelled from the TUC. Soon after it split, with the left-wingers forming an alternative union called the EPIU, which later merged with the T&G.

The TUC general secretary, Norman Willis, was working as hard as he could to persuade union members that things were never going to be the same. The Conservatives had been re-elected in June 1983, having won the votes of millions of ordinary workers. There was a wide gap between the union leadership and what your ordinary worker did and said.

There was a general feeling among union members that Margaret Thatcher was out to destroy the movement. Although there were about ten million union members, it was as if we didn't exist. I remember Bill Morris saying to me once, 'We're not some campaign. We're part of civil society.' Thatcher treated the trade unions with contempt. She had taken on the miners in a year-long dispute over pit closures. Despite a highly organized strike campaign led by Arthur Scargill, which saw running battles between miners and the police, she won when the National Coal Board effectively, area by area, starved the miners out so that they would return to their jobs. I didn't have much time for Scargill. I thought he had a huge ego and by adopting an aggressive and confrontational approach had handled the miners' strike badly.

But I hated what Margaret Thatcher's government were doing. I thought it was heartless to make so many people unemployed. True, new technology was changing working practices, but I felt the government should have invested more money in retraining workers. People were just abandoned and left to join the dole queue.

Thatcher's weakening of union power had also seriously weakened Labour. Neil Kinnock was attempting to reform the Labour Party and appeal to a wider section of voters. He knew this was the only way it stood any chance of returning to government. However the party was split between those who supported Kinnock and the Militant Tendency.

On the Saturday afternoon of TUC conference week I played for the TUC general council cricket team against the press at an old army barracks just outside Blackpool. I was the first woman to do this. I was roped in because the team was short of players.

Bill Sirs, general secretary of the steel workers' union, said. 'Come on. You're always arguing about equality. We need a player.'

I didn't get an opportunity to bowl. I just had to field, and I made sure I stood as far away from the ball as I could get. Towards the end of the game, I went out to bat, clad in pads. I stood there at the crease swinging the bat and, somehow, I managed to score four runs. This meant that I didn't disgrace myself. The Co-op Bank and Unity Trust Bank had provided refreshments. Many spectators started drinking early, so by the time the game began lots of them were very much the worse for wear.

One of the biggest obstacles faced by working women is childcare. As a working mother, I knew how important this was. Few employers provided crèches, and nurseries were expensive. When I had worked at CDP, I had got involved in a campaign to force Southwark Council to honour its pledge to build a nursery on a piece of land near the Elephant and Castle. We persuaded UCATT, the construction workers' union, to boycott the site until Southwark agreed to do what it had promised. In the end, the money for the nursery was withdrawn by the government when the GLC was abolished. One of my most significant achievements as national women's officer was persuading the management at a pharmaceutical factory and at Joyce Green Hospital in Dartford to establish a nursery between them.

Women's health has always been an issue for politically active women. So I ran a campaign to alert women to the dangers of cervical cancer. At this time, around 12,000 women a year were dying from the disease. The Women's National Cancer Control Campaign ran a mobile unit that toured factories and other workplaces to provide women with screening and information. This meant women could have tests during work time and they could go with their friends. It wasn't difficult to persuade companies to take part in the scheme. We made a short film in which women at the Halfords factory in the Midlands talked about how the screening had identified cancerous cells. I'm sure many lives were saved.

I began to feel that I was making progress in the job. As an official attending the executive council, I could present the concerns of women up and down the country to the members. They might not agree with everything I said, but at least I could try and discuss the issues in a rational way with them.

While Ron had supported Bill's idea of giving women a voice on the regional committees and setting up a quarterly magazine, when it came down to issues such as pay he couldn't grasp that women were not being treated the same as men by the union. When a group of women employed by the Freemans mail-order company asked the T&G to support their claim for equal pay he refused. I was furious when I heard this and asked to see him.

'Look, Ron, we're spending more than a million pounds on an employment tribunal case for dockers whose jobs have gone. Yet we're not spending a single penny on supporting women, who make up a huge part of the labour market.'

'Well, the Equal Opportunities Commission does this kind of thing,' he said, leaning back in his chair.

'But these women pay their dues to the T&G like the men do.'

Ron stood up and stared absentmindedly out of the window. 'I'm sorry,' he murmured.

I continued to argue with him, but he wouldn't budge. I could see he was embarrassed. I think he felt he couldn't backtrack on his decision. I left his office, slamming the door behind me, feeling frustrated and hugely disappointed in him.

The women at Freemans took their case to the Equal Opportunities Commission and it went all the way to the House of Lords. Because the women were T&G members I decided to go there to hear the decision. I sat in the public gallery in the chamber with a number of the Freemans women. The officials from the Equal Opportunities Commission were pretty offhand with me, as they saw it as their case and nothing to do with the union. When one of the Law Lords announced that the court had found in favour of the women, they leapt up from their seats, cheering and hugging each other. I was delighted for the women, but at the same time I didn't think the ruling was going to make much impact on the attitude of those at the top of the unions who believed that industrial relations should only be concerned with men and that the law had no place in setting wages.

I was reminded of this when I organized an equal pay conference at Transport House. The chair of the Equal Opportunities Commission was coming to speak. Although the Equal Pay Act had taken effect in 1975, many employers simply regraded women's jobs so that they didn't have to pay them more. I was so nervous about it that the night before I had a dream in which everyone was in a panic because the coffee machine didn't work. On the morning of the conference I bumped into the national secretary of the food and drink committee in the corridor. As it represented huge numbers of women working in food manufacturing companies, breweries and restaurants, I asked him if he was going to attend.

'I've got industrial matters to deal with,' he said.

'What do you mean?' I said, unable to believe what I was hearing. I wouldn't have asked the secretary for the dockers if he was going to the meeting, because they had hardly any female members. But there were tens of thousands of women members in the food and drink industry.

'I'm busy.'

'Isn't women's pay is an industrial issue?'

'I'm interested in getting fair pay for all our members. Not just women.'

I was speechless. I returned to my office, thinking that, while I had made some progress in my fight for women to be represented fairly in the T&G and given the same rights as men, I still had a major battle on my hands. But one thing was for sure, I wasn't giving up.

8. Don't Wear Any Make-Up

As THE PLANE DESCENDED through the clouds I pressed my face to the cabin window and caught glimpses of mountains below, ringing the sprawling city of Santiago. I felt a thrill run through me, but at the same time I have to admit that I was a little nervous. It was March 1986 and Chile was in the grip of the dictator General Augusto Pinochet who, assisted and encouraged by the United States, had led a military coup in 1973 and overthrown the democratically elected government of Dr Salvador Allende.

Allende's government had introduced radical policies, among them taking Chile's natural resources out of the hands of US companies and nationalizing them, establishing a welfare state and introducing a programme of land reform. But his economic policies led to soaring inflation and food shortages. Lorry-owners staged a strike to oppose his plans for nationalization. This political turmoil was exactly what the US wanted, as they didn't like the idea of a socialist state in their backyard.

Pinochet dealt brutally with those who opposed him. Tens of thousands of people were tortured and killed, with many more imprisoned. Others fled abroad. The trade-union movement in Britain adopted political prisoners and campaigned for their release. I had been invited by the Chile Solidarity Campaign, set up after the coup, to join a celebration for International Women's Day and to meet some of the women who were engaged in struggle against the repression of the government.

This wasn't my first trip overseas as a senior union official. In 1985 I'd flown to Madrid to take part in the women's conference organized by the International Confederation of Free Trade Unions. I was part of the TUC delegation but, although I had been elected to the general council, I hadn't, as Ann Gibson put it, 'gone through the sausage machine yet'. In other words, I hadn't gone through all the necessary bureaucratic procedures. This was the first international conference I'd attended.

What struck me was that, compared with most countries in Europe, the UK was quite progressive where women's rights were concerned. The UK had introduced the Sex Discrimination Act and set up the Equal Opportunities Commission. What's more, women in the trade-union movement were lobbying the Labour Party to ensure that every shortlist in a parliamentary constituency to elect a new MP contained at least one woman. It was a different story in many other parts of Europe.

I don't remember much else about the conference in Spain except that the US delegation made an official complaint to the organizers about our behaviour, accusing us of singing Communist songs in the bar of the hotel where all the delegates stayed. I think we were singing, 'I Dreamed I Saw Joe Hill Last Night', a popular song in the labour movement.

But this was my first trip to Latin America. I was travelling with Jane McKay, chair of the T&G national women's advisory committee and a member of Chile Solidarity Scotland, and several other women union officials. We had decided to take five hundred pounds with us in order to buy equipment for the Chilean trade unions, which were still illegal. Pinochet's economic policies had pushed half the population below the poverty line. Jane was also carrying a suitcase with various medical supplies, which someone she knew had donated from a hospital where she worked.

At Santiago airport we were met by a group of women activists, all smiling and holding out huge bunches of flowers. Under a clear blue sky, we travelled by car into the centre of the city, passing through some run-down suburbs. Several times we got stuck behind a ramshackle and dirty bus, belching out black smoke.

Our hotel was cosy and situated close to the Metropolitan Cathedral, in a part of the city containing a mixture of modern office blocks and Spanish colonial-style buildings set in leafy streets. Christine Crawley, member of the European Parliament for Birmingham East, arrived that evening and we all enjoyed an excellent dinner in the hotel restaurant. After flying 7,000 miles, I was exhausted and I went to sleep as soon as my head hit the pillow.

During the next few days we met various groups of women and learnt how dire the economic situation was. Many women wanted to work to help support their families, but there were few jobs. One day, I met a group of women who were learning to be sewing-machinists in order to make clothes to sell in the markets. I was so moved that I told them when I returned to London I would raise £1,000 for them so that they could buy machines and materials. I planned to ask each member on the T&G general council to contribute £20. But I didn't have to, because when I spoke to Ron Todd to ask permission to do this, he gave me the money himself, which was incredibly generous of him.

We met lots of families in different parts of the city. One evening, we went for supper with a family who had left Chile and settled in Scotland after Pinochet came to power. Jane was good friends with them because she had helped find them a house and jobs. I found it very amusing listening to their children speaking English with a broad Scottish accent.

One day we took a taxi to the foot of the Andes to meet a group of fruit-pickers. We arrived in an area that consisted of rows of what looked like garden sheds. The locals made their living from harvesting plums, apples and grapes. When the fruit-pickers emerged from their huts the first thing I noticed was that they were all dressed incredibly smartly. We sat with them in the sunshine under a large tree and they told us about their working conditions and pay. They had no set hours. They just had to continue working until all the fruit was picked. As I listened to them, I thought to myself that this was like slave labour.

We met with men who had been taken from Santiago to the south of the country, thousands of miles away, and dumped by the roadside. The regime thought they would be abandoned there, maybe die or at least learn a lesson and not cause trouble again. Most people outside Santiago were unaware of the seriousness of the political situation, or that people were being arrested and executed. As the men made the long journey back to Santiago they stopped in villages along the way, where they told people what was happening in the capital.

I met a group of the lorry-owners who had gone on strike in 1973, nearly bringing the country to a halt. Farmers had been unable to deliver their produce and shops soon ran out of everything. This had led, ultimately, to Pinochet seizing power. I wanted to find out what they now thought of their action.

'Do you regret it?' I asked.

'Yes. We didn't expect the country to turn out the way it has,' said a tall man with jet-black hair. He was one of the most handsome men I had ever met, and I found my mind wandering.

We met several groups of women running soup kitchens in shanty towns. Most were from the domestic servants' union and the street sellers' union. They were helped by Mapuche women and women from the mining regions of southern Chile.

One of the most moving moments of my trip was when we met some of the mothers of the disappeared. As I sat there listening to their stories and looking at the photos of their sons, daughters and husbands each of them clutched, I felt tears well up in my eyes. I asked myself how I would feel if any of my children had been taken away and I had no way of knowing where they were or even whether they were still alive. If your child dies, then at least that gives you some closure. But these women didn't know if their children were alive or not. They might have felt in the back of their minds that their loved ones were dead, but they didn't have any proof. I'd read about these mothers, but it was only now that I really grasped something of the terrible emotional pain that they were going through. When Christine, Jane and I came out of the centre to get into the car waiting for us none of us could speak. It was all too much for us.

At another community centre we joined a group of women cutting up ribbons in the colours of the Chilean flag in preparation for the International Women's Day celebration a few days later. It had been organized by women from various groups on the broad left of Chilean politics, including the Socialist Bloc, the Radical Party, the Christian Democrats, the Popular Democratic Movement, the Revolutionary Left Movement, feminists and others.

'Carry a shopping bag with you,' said one of the women.

'Why?' I asked.

'Because if there is trouble from the police or the army you can then walk away as if you are going shopping.'

'Don't wear any make-up,' said another woman.

'No?' I said.

She shook her head. 'Put Vaseline on your face instead, as this will protect you from the burning sensation tear gas produces.'

'Tear gas?'

'Yes.'

None of us had thought about facing tear gas, which we should have done, given the reputation of the police and the army in Chile.

We were shown a list of the interrogation centres and police stations to which we might he taken if we were arrested.

When I was sitting at home in London, the thought of taking part in a march in Santiago didn't worry me. I had gone on lots of demonstrations. At Grunwick I had seen police on horses charge the crowd. I had learnt that if you stayed on the edge you were usually all right. It was the people in the middle who normally got arrested. But now I was beginning to feel scared. And I could tell from the expressions on the faces of the others in the delegation that they felt the same. But we all knew that, because our participation in the event meant so much to the Chilean women whom we had met, there was no way we could not take part. We had to stand alongside them. They would still be struggling long after we had returned to Britain.

On the day of the celebration, we made our way to a park, where we met with about forty other women from Italy, Denmark, France and other countries. Each of us held a small Chilean flag, we linked arms in a circle and began singing the Internationale as loudly as we could and set off towards the starting-point of the march. It wasn't long before we saw groups of soldiers with blackened faces dressed in full combat gear and carrying machine-guns. They looked pretty menacing.

All of a sudden, I could hear a heavy rumbling sound in the distance. It got louder. And then I heard shouting. Through the trees I could see several tanks and small vans that appeared to be spraying something.

'It's tear gas!' shouted Christine.

We hadn't put any Vaseline on our faces, as we were recommended to do, because we didn't have any. But we had made sure not to put on any mascara.

We all decided to stick together in threes and make a run for it. I was with Christine and Jane, who were both much taller then me, and when we linked arms and ran my feet hardly touched the ground. Although we were frightened we burst into laughter. It must have looked comical.

For the next three hours we followed the marchers, who were reforming into small groups around the park. We watched as barricades were placed across the roads and groups of young people began walking in front of the traffic. The air was filled with beeping car horns and people chanting, 'He will fall! He will fall!' Then a huge water cannon appeared, spewing forth filthy, stinking water at everyone.

As dusk began to fall, we were told by one of the organizers that the police brutality would increase dramatically as night drew on, so it would be best for us to return to our hotel.

'Last night, the police went into some districts of the city and began shooting. They did this to intimidate people, so that they wouldn't demonstrate,' she said.

Helen Garner and Diane Dixon, who worked for the Chile Solidarity Campaign, joined us and we set off quickly in the direction of the main shopping area. But we soon realised that we didn't have a clue which direction the hotel was in. Every time we stopped at a junction to try and work out where we were, we noticed that a smartly dressed man in his forties did the same. This seemed odd.

'He's following us,' I said.

We didn't know what to do. As we stood at a set of traffic lights, surrounded by crowds of protesters, I heard someone call out in English. A very intellectual-looking woman with shaggy hair appeared at our side. She turned out to be Joan Jara, a British woman who had been married to Victor Jara, a folk-singer and activist. Joan had been a dancer and knew Diane through the Chile Solidarity Campaign. Joan led us through some back streets to her flat. I looked around but couldn't see the smartly dressed man anywhere. At her flat we spent a couple of hours listening to her tell us about how bad the situation in Chile was. She described how Victor had been arrested one night and taken to a football stadium, where his fingers were chopped off and then he was executed. I was horrified by what I heard.

That night in the hotel I reflected on how, thirteen years after the fascist coup which had destroyed democracy in Chile, Pinochet still was not taking any chances. Apparently, a group of women in a park presented a serious threat to him.

The recurrent theme of the Chilean women's message to us, everywhere we went, was: 'Tell them about us back in Europe. Tell them about the struggle we are engaged in. And, above all, thank them for their solidarity. Without it we would not have the courage to continue.'

Soon after I arrived back in London, Helen gave me a video of the demonstration. Her husband, who worked for the BBC, had been given it by someone in Santiago. I watched it with Jane McKay. We saw scenes of the police charging demonstrators. At one point, they fired the water canon at a woman who was thrown against a wall, splitting her head open. We hadn't realized exactly how violent the situation had been. We were both glad to be back in the comfort of my front room.

I returned to Chile two-and-a-half years later with Joan Ruddock, MP for Lewisham Deptford, after the plebiscite that had started to bring down the curtain on Pinochet's rule. The scars of his dictatorship were still very visible, from the bullet holes in the walls of a community centre to the abject poverty of the people on the streets and in the shanty towns. The United States had a lot to answer for. Chile had had the oldest democracy in Latin America. The fact was that the US government couldn't stomach the thought of left-wingers in their backyard.

Another country that attracted the support of the trade-union movement back then was Palestine. I made my first visit there in 1987 when I was part of a delegation of women organized by Palestinian Trade Union Friends. We were to meet Palestinian women living in the West Bank to learn about their struggles and life under Israeli occupation. This was the time of the first intifada, or uprising.

I arrived at Heathrow Airport early in the morning. Jane McKay and several other women were already there, along with Yussef, the London organizer of Palestinian Trade Union Friends.

After we had checked our suitcases in, Yussef handed Jane an envelope.

'What's this?' she said.

'Something to help our brothers and sisters back home,' he said.

Jane looked at me with an expression that said, 'What should I do?'

We knew the envelope must contain money, probably from well-off Palestinians or other Arabs. I didn't know what to say. I could see that we were all concerned about taking cash into Israel. If we were discovered, we might end up in serious hot water.

'Don't worry,' said Yussef. 'Someone will meet you at your hotel in Jerusalem. Give him the envelope.'

With this, he said a cheery goodbye and left us. We sat down to discuss what to do. Jane was worried about what might happen if she was searched by Israeli security. We all agreed that this was a real possibility. Jane then got up and disappeared to the ladies'. When she returned, she handed each of us an envelope.

'I've divided the money between us. This way, if any of us is stopped, we can just say it's spending money.'

It seemed a good solution, but, all the same, I still felt anxious. Why would a trade-union delegate be carrying a thousand pounds for a seven-day trip to Palestine? I wasn't sure this would wash with security.

By the time we landed in Tel Aviv, I felt extremely nervous, as there were so many police officers and soldiers patrolling the airport. The worst part was going through passport control. I felt guilty carrying the money and wondered if this showed on my face. I felt a huge relief when the customs officer stamped my passport and waved me though.

We checked into our hotel, which was in a busy street in East Jerusalem, the Arab part of the city. At breakfast in the restaurant the following morning we were discussing what to do about the money, which was in Jane's handbag, when a man wearing a dark suit and sunglasses came towards us.

'Which of you is Jane?' he asked.

'I am,' said Jane.

'Yussef mentioned me, I believe.'

'That's right,' said Jane, a little unsure.

'Please follow me,' he said, turning towards the door.

After breakfast we waited in the hotel lobby for Jane to return. As the time ticked by, we were starting to get worried. She didn't know the man she had gone off with. What if she had been kidnapped? She didn't come back until nearly lunchtime. She told us the man had driven her to a house somewhere, where she was introduced to another man, to whom she gave the money. We all thought the experience was bizarre.

After lunch, Rashid, a member of the transport union, arrived at the hotel in a white minibus to drive us to a nursery school in the West Bank. Under a piercing, cold sun, we rattled and bounced our way along a narrow, pot-holed road, passing brown and green fields of olive trees and grazing sheep. The landscape soon became very hilly and rocky. Half-finished buildings seemed to be everywhere. Rashid pointed to a housing development on a hill and told us it was a Jewish settlement.

Suddenly he slowed down and said, 'Passports.'

Ahead of us stood a group of heavily armed soldiers alongside a tank and an armoured car. One of them stood in the middle of the road and flagged us down, his machine-gun pointed directly at us. He ordered us all out of the minibus and told us to stand in a row. Another soldier then asked each of us for our passports. As he was inspecting them, I noticed other soldiers heaving our bags out of the minibus and dumping them on the ground. I thought this seemed a bit unnecessary, as we were only a bunch of middle-aged female trade-union officials from Britain. By any stretch of the imagination, we didn't look like potential terrorists. The soldiers left Rashid to repack our bags. I felt this was a silent insult.

We eventually arrived in a dusty village of white houses. Rashid led us towards a group of buildings which contained a nursery and, above it, workshops.

One of the teachers showed us around, explaining how important it was that the children were taught Palestinian history. The workshops had been established for young women whose fathers had been killed in the troubles. We watched women learning needlework, lacemaking, hairdressing and other new skills so that they could support their families. Some of the goods were for sale, so we bought lace and tablecloths.

'Why is it that all the images of Palestine on TV are negative?' the teacher asked us.

'Well, the media always seem to want to show the worst images they can find,' I said. It was true. So often the news gives you a distorted picture of a country.

We then visited a refugee camp and a primary school, where I was amazed to find children learning maths in English. Because there was no heating as a result of daily power cuts, they all sat there wearing hats and gloves.

I also met a family in a small village who used to earn a living from growing olive trees.

'See here,' said the husband, pointing to a piece of scrubland. 'This is where our trees grew.'

'What happened?' I said.

'One day, the soldiers came and cut them down.' He opened the palms of his hands. 'Now we have nothing.'

I sensed a repressed anger in him. All he had to support his family had been taken away from him. I too felt angry. What right did the army have to take away a person's livelihood? How was this family meant to survive?

One morning, Hanan Ashrawi, then a peace campaigner and political activist and later a Palestinian minister, came to see us at our hotel. Over coffee and iced water, she explained the political situation to us.

'There will be no peace until both Palestinians and Israelis sit down together and agree that the rights of each people have to be respected.'

'Do you think it will happen?' I asked.

'I hope so,' she said. 'Violence is not the answer.'

In Nablus we met the head of all the trade unions in Palestine and he invited us for lunch on Sunday with his father, who owned a butcher's shop. We had to go through lots of narrow alleyways to get to his father's house. All the women were in one room and all the men were in another. We had a wonderful meal of roast lamb with almonds.

Afterwards, we were walking through the town, when I heard someone shouting in the distance. I looked around to see several soldiers running towards us.

'What's the matter with them?' I asked.

'Let's hurry up,' said Jane.

We began walking faster, and the shouting got louder. Eventually they caught up with us and motioned us to stand against the wall of a house.

I took out my passport. 'English. We're English,' I said, holding it in the air.

A soldier took it from me and examined it. 'OK,' he said and waved us on.

Experiences like this gave me an insight into what daily life must be life for ordinary Palestinians. It seemed that the Israelis were determined to disrupt their lives as much as possible.

Although we had a busy schedule, we found time to visit the Old City in Jerusalem. As we made our way through its narrow, crowded streets, I felt I was back in the Middle Ages. We stood at the Wailing Wall, watching bearded Jewish men inserting prayers written on small pieces of paper into cracks between the stones.

We also crossed into West Jerusalem, the Jewish part of the city. It looked very different. The streets were better maintained and the shops and buildings smarter. It was more like London. Israeli citizens had the kind of freedom that everyone has a right to expect.

I felt outraged at the way the Palestinian people were treated. It was unfair. I kept thinking of that man standing beside the ground where his olive trees had once grown. Of course, Israel has the right to live in peace, but this shouldn't be at the expense of the human rights of the Palestinians.

I was now spending more and more time travelling. I had to attend various conferences each year. Two of the most important were the TUC women's conference and the Labour Party women's conference. Each time, I always came away feeling invigorated. As with any conference, the speakers were always a mixed bunch. But what I really enjoyed was the opportunity to chat with other women activists over a meal or in the bar in the evening, and see how everyone grew in confidence when they listened to MPs such as Jo Richardson, Audrey Wise and Renée Short give stirring speeches.

At each Labour women's conference, we organized a cabaret in the bar of one of the hotels. We would do things like pretending we were on the TUC general council and telling all the men to piss off. Some of us would do impersonations of union leaders. Glenys Kinnock and I dressed up as men. It was hilarious. But Neil Kinnock insisted on calling everyone 'love': 'Well done, love.' 'Very good, love.' He really wound up all the women.

Mind you, attending conferences often meant staying in crummy hotels or bed and breakfasts and eating terrible food in windy seaside resorts. One year, I attended five conferences in Blackpool. That was enough to last a lifetime.

In 1986 I had been appointed to the Equal Opportunities Commission, set up after the Sex Discrimination Act in 1975, so I was now travelling by train to its office in Manchester once a month. Appointments to the Equal Opportunities Commission were made by the Secretary of State. At that time, three seats were allocated to the TUC, three to the CBI and the rest to various other people.

I also now sat on the executive council of the Confederation of Shipbuilding and Engineering Unions, known as the Confed, and based at Walworth Road, next to the Labour Party offices. Our meetings, however, were usually held at a hotel in Southampton Row, near Russell Square. The Confed was unsurprisingly a very male organization, what I called the horny-handed sons of toil, an expression I picked up from my dad.

The Confed, which was over 100 years old, had once been very powerful, having negotiated a single pay agreement with all the engineering companies. But by the 1980s its influence and importance were waning, as shipyards and engineering companies across the country began to close. The union executive, however, understood that all the blame couldn't be pinned on the Thatcher government. New technology was changing the workplace and you couldn't turn the clock back.

I felt at home on the Confed council, although it was a while before the other members took me seriously, even though they were always very gentlemanly. I've always felt that men behave differently in mixed company. That's one reason why more women in decision-making are a good thing. But they didn't have much time for women's issues. If I pointed out that in union-organized workplaces men and women got the same pay for the same job, but women didn't have access to the more highly paid jobs, the others on the committee just raised their eyebrows and then moved on.

The committee members were essentially a bunch of fixers. Although the unions and bosses might seem to be at loggerheads publicly, behind the scenes things were often more cordial. The officials and management would engage in a formal discussion around the table and then go off together afterwards and have 'a knife and fork', meaning going out to dinner with the employer and sorting it all out. These were very professional trade unionists who had been at the game a long time. The last thing they wanted was a strike, because they knew that once you got the workers out on strike you then had to get them back to work. Apart from anything else, bringing the workers out on strike costs a union a lot of money. It has to pay strike pay. Instead they would use tactics such as work-to-rule.

The Confed ran a campaign for a thirty-five-hour week. When it had asked every member to pay an extra 10p a week to fund any strike that might be called, so much money came in and so little of it was spent that it was put into a trust. Today, there must be several million pounds in it.

I will never forget attending my first Confed annual conference in Llandudno. All the delegates were meant to sit with their groups in seats set out in rows in front of the platform, where the executive sat.

When I arrived, Tom Crispin, the national secretary for the power and engineering sector and leader of the T&G delegation, came up to me and said, 'Your seat is at the end.'

'OK,' I said, and made my way to the far end of the table.

Afterwards, Freddy Howell, a national power and engineering officer, came up to me and said, 'He shouldn't have done that.'

'What do you mean?'

'You were supposed to sit at this end of the table with the other national officials.'

I laughed and thought how childish it was of Tom Crispin to play such a daft trick. I was also annoyed with myself for falling for it. So I said to myself, 'I'll show you. Just you wait.'

I went to Llandudno for the Confed annual conference every year. We all travelled there on the Saturday or Sunday and booked into the Imperial Hotel. The executive committee would meet on Monday from 10.00 a.m. until 11.30 a.m. and then that was it for the day. The conference opened on Tuesday morning when the president gave an address and notices would be read out. This never took much longer than an hour and a half. On Wednesdays and Thursdays there would be sessions in the mornings and afternoons.

When the members stood at the rostrum they never seemed to make proper speeches but just told stories or jokes instead. I can remember Jimmy Airlie, national officer with the engineering workers' union, and a rough and tough Glaswegian, telling a joke about a young lad on a Youth Training Scheme who had to fill in a form each week to show what he was doing and then hand it in to the office. His occupation had been described as 'excavating excrement'. But he wrote 'shovelling shit'. He wrote this each time for a few weeks and then was told that the girls in the office were offended. 'Write "excavating excrement" instead,' he was ordered. The boy said, 'If I could spell that I wouldn't be shovelling shit.'

I sometimes wondered if the real purpose of the conference was to have a good booze-up. Many of the members drank like fish and would often leave the executive meeting at the hotel in Southampton Row and spend the afternoon in the pub. I never went with them, as I wouldn't have been able to work for the rest of the day. During the conference in Llandudno, the Imperial Hotel had what was known as 'the president's cocktail bar', which was really a free bar until about 5.00 p.m. As soon as the morning session finished the members would all head there.

By the evening it was impossible to have a conversation with anyone because they were all drunk and loud. One night I went out for dinner with some friends and, when I came back to the hotel, some of the executive members called me over to the bar and asked me to have a drink.

'Come on, Margaret. Just a quick one,' said Nigel Harris, who was a big guy, from the engineering and construction sector.

'OK. I'll have a gin and tonic, then.' I didn't really want a drink, but I thought I had better be sociable.

He ordered the drink and then realized he didn't have any money on him.

'Tell you what,' he said to the barmaid, 'put it on Gavin Laird's bill.' Gavin was the general secretary of the engineers. The other members saw him as nothing more than a clerk. The president was the top dog. The general secretary was seen as the run-around. Gavin was very smart.

I said, 'I'm going to leave you to it, Nigel,' thinking the whole scene was very comical, and slipped off to bed.

Most of the committee had left school at fifteen and gone into apprenticeships. They were very streetwise, and they knew how to negotiate, but they struggled to express themselves in the archaic and stilted language that characterized meetings. The general secretary of the Confed was Alex Ferry, an unassuming but very clever man, even though he hadn't received much of a formal education. Part of his job was to travel around the country visiting companies. When he gave you an account of a meeting he had attended, you felt that you had been there yourself. I remember the time when I was travelling with the T&G delegation back to London and Alex expressed concern that we were leaving the engineering members and they would all get drunk. Given their reputation for serious drinking, I'm sure they did.

Since 1947 dockers had been covered by the National Dock Labour Scheme, which, in effect, guaranteed many dockers jobs for life. But in 1989 the Employment Secretary, Norman Fowler, abolished it, claiming it stood in the way of modernization. The dockers came out on strike, but those in Hull, Southampton and Felixstowe soon started returning to work because they didn't want to lose their jobs. The Tilbury dockers, however, stayed out on strike.

One day Ron called us all into the chamber at Transport House in Smith Square and announced that, following an executive meeting, support for the Tilbury dockers was being withdrawn. The T&G couldn't continue to support a strike that didn't have the backing of the majority of the members.

A group of dockers were across the road in the Marquis of Granby pub at the time. When news reached them about Ron's decision, they headed over to Transport House, bursting through the doors of the chamber, shouting and swearing. They ignored Ron's plea for order and began walking around the chamber, trying to intimidate the officials. I was sitting next to the secretary for Region Two, which covered Southampton. One of the dockers leaned over him and was about to thump him when George Wright stood in front of him. I thought to myself, I'm glad I'm a woman, because no one is going to hit me.

In 1990 I went on what was known as 'the CIA tour' when I flew out to Washington, DC. The US embassy in

London arranged this, the idea being to try to win the support of people it regarded as influential in British politics. I travelled with Kay Carberry, head of the equal rights department at the TUC. It was a fascinating trip. Among other things, we met senior officials from the American Federation of Labor, and visited the vast Ford car factory in Detroit and a museum in Washington dedicated to the trade-union movement. One of the things I remember most is being picked up at Minneapolis–St Paul airport by an elderly construction union official in a huge burgundy stretch limo and then taken for a meal at a revolving restaurant with a spectacular view across the city and the Mississippi river.

It was around this time that I received the news that Joe had died. I hadn't had any contact with him since he went into residential care in 1974. I thought long and hard about whether or not I should go to his funeral, but I decided to go would be hypocritical. Carol and Stella went, but Jeffrey didn't, as he still felt angry with Joe. But I felt sad over his death. His life hadn't been easy.

I felt I was beginning to make progress in getting women's issues on to the T&G agenda. One day, Sid Staden complimented me on my work.

'I do believe you're coming round to the idea of equality, Sid,' I said.

'Margaret, I'm recognizing the bleeding inevitable.'

'Oh, well, still some way to go,' I replied.

Of course, there were still many in the union who didn't think that getting a fair deal for women was important. In particular, I found Tom Crispin, the national secretary of the power and engineering group—the man who had told me that my seat was at the end—difficult to work with. On one occasion he invited me to a pay conference in the hall at Transport House because I had responsibility for white-collar workers in the engineering sector.

He said to me in the meeting, 'You explain what you think about the pay offer.'

I knew he had done this because he didn't like me and the work I was doing and he knew that I wasn't familiar with the pay system in engineering. There was no way I was going to make myself look an idiot, so I said, 'Do you know what? I feel as if I am being asked to do a maths degree when I still haven't learnt my two-times table. So I think we'll leave it like that.'

Jim Hunt, the regional secretary for the Midlands, which was the heart of the engineering industry, was very hostile to the national women's committee. He once said to me that having a women's organizer in the region was a 'job in the ghetto'. He saw it as a meaningless post. I said there was a secretary in his region for power and engineering, one for textiles and another for the vehicle-building industry and so on. Given that these were also single-issue areas, were they also jobs in the ghetto? Jim became a good friend eventually. Years later, when he retired, he sent me a card that said, 'I know I didn't always get it right, but I got there in the end.' He ended up running a very good women's programme in his region.

During my eight years as national women's officer the structure of the workforce changed enormously. Throughout the 1980s many of our traditional members, such as bus conductors, tin miners in Cornwall, general engineers, steelworkers, textile-workers and workers in shipyards, lost their jobs, and our membership in what had been our traditional base of support began to slump. On the other hand, more part-time jobs were being created, many of them done by women. All of this, plus other changes in society, pushed the women's agenda forward.

The longer I was in the job the more I saw the confidence of women at the local level grow. Many were now prepared to take on their all-powerful regional secretaries. One woman, who worked as a shop steward at Pendelton's ice cream factory in the north-west, encouraged many workers to join the union by talking to them about their entitlement to benefits. When Pendelton's closed, she went off to university and obtained a degree.

Stories like this drove me on to do much more. I could feel things changing, but I knew there was still some way to go before women would achieve full equality in the T&G with men.

9. On the Shop Floor

WHEN A VACANCY for national organizer, the third most senior post in the T&G after the general secretary and the deputy general secretary, was advertised in *The Record*, the T&G newspaper, Bill said to me, 'You have to apply.' I could tell that he wanted me to get the job and was letting me know that there was a very good chance I would. This is how most appointments in the T&G were made back then. It was all done by a nod and a wink.

Bill had succeeded Ron Todd as general secretary. We had held a farewell party for Ron at Walthamstow town hall, attended by officials from all the major unions. His mother, who was ninety, played the piano. Behind her on the stage was a rug someone had made with Ron's face on it. I thought this was hilarious. Before he left, Ron gave me several photos of women union members in the 1940s, which I hung on the wall of my office.

Ron had been criticized by some of the regional secretaries for wasting the union's money. The last year he was general secretary the union spent £4 million more than its income, creating a huge financial problem. When Bill was appointed general secretary the first thing he did was to sort out the financial mess. To reduce the union's expenditure, he brought in Peter Reignier as national finance director. The eleven regions were reduced to eight, which meant that the number of officials employed was smaller. The three regional secretaries who lost their jobs were given a generous redundancy package. Bill nominated George Wright, his arch-enemy, for a vacancy on a TUC committee in Brussels. This was to keep him sweet. A central payment system was introduced and contracts with solicitors renegotiated. The regional secretaries didn't like Peter Reignier, because he knew more about their finances than they did.

The interview for national organizer was held in the chamber at Transport House. I sat in the middle, facing Bill, Jack Adams, the deputy general secretary, and Ray Collins, the central office manager, who were all sitting on a platform. Behind me sat the members of the general council. It was very disconcerting, a bit like being in a court. But I gave a good interview, answering all the questions well and showing that I was every bit as capable as the other candidates, who were national officials and regional officials. Bill was right: I got the job.

I took up the post in September 1992, feeling proud that I was the first woman in the T&G at such a senior level. I agreed to combine it with my previous post of national women's officer until a replacement was found. This wasn't an ideal situation, as it meant that I couldn't give my full attention to my new job. I was relieved when, a few months later, Diana Holland was appointed as national women's officer.

As national organizer, my remit was not just women but union members as a whole. My main role was to organize campaigns to recruit new members. Like most unions, the T&G had seen its membership decline dramatically in the previous twenty years. I also became secretary of the national co-ordinating committee, which decided on recruitment policies for all the regions to follow.

There was a fierce rivalry between the different trade unions. Each of us wanted to boost our own membership and didn't want someone joining another union. The Thatcher government introduced legislation which allowed a person to join any union they wanted, making the TUC's 1939 Bridlington Agreement, forbidding one union to steal members from another, unenforceable. For example, if you were a local government worker, you could choose to join the T&G, the GMB or Unison. An employer could decide which union to allow in the workplace. When some members of Unison in the north fell out with the union and joined the T&G,

the T&G complained to the TUC. Instead of having to hand members back, Unison were fined.

Despite the miners' strike, the Conservative government had gone ahead with its pit closure programme, destroying the coal-mining industry, decimating communities and leaving tens of thousands of men without a job. It was hard to believe that during the Second World War there were over a million miners in Britain and nearly 1,000 pits. John Major had now succeeded Margaret Thatcher as the Tory leader, after she was ousted in November 1990. I had only been in my new post a couple of weeks when Michael Heseltine, the president of the board of trade, announced that up to thirty-one out of the fifty remaining deep mines faced closure. This would result in the loss of 31,000 jobs.

The TUC decided to hold a march through central London to protest at the government's plan, and I had the job of organizing support from all the T&G regions. Each region organized its own coaches, but I had to make sure that this was done properly and that everyone knew where to park in London, how to get to the meeting-point for the march and where to get the banners. I also had to help organize trains from some parts of the country. It was a massive exercise.

The march began in Hyde Park and ended in Trafalgar Square, where Norman Willis, Bill Morris, Mick McGahey and Arthur Scargill all made speeches. It was one of the biggest union demonstrations ever seen in central London. We were joined by many non-union members, mainly middle-class professionals, drawn to take part by what John Monks called 'the magic of the miners'. It poured down with rain, but everyone stayed the course.

Not long after the march, I was part of a TUC delegation that met Heseltine at his office in Victoria Street. He came across as very suave and confident and, like so many seasoned politicians, gave very little away. We asked him what he planned to do about the communities these closures would affect. He trotted out the usual stuff about training programmes, quoting sums of money that would be made available. But it was all very vague. We left, knowing that, when it came to it, nothing concrete would be done to help those miners who were going to lose their jobs. The truth was that most would end up in the dole queue.

The government also decided to do away with 'check off', where employers deducted union contributions from wages. When they ended check off on the railways union membership plummeted, The Conservatives introduced a law that meant every ten years union members had to sign a document to say that they agreed to their dues being deducted from their wages. This was another way they were trying to break the power of the unions.

I had the task of co-ordinating efforts to persuade T&G members to sign up again. We ran a massive campaign and went to nearly every workplace where we had members to make sure everyone agreed again to have the contributions collected by the employer. Everyone had to sign a piece of paper to say this. It was an administrative nightmare and took up huge amounts of time, and it wasn't made any easier by the outdated computer system we had at Transport House.

But the scheme backfired on the Tories, because when union officials visited workplaces to collect signatures, someone would say, 'Those workers over there aren't in the union,' and we would gain new members.

Falling membership continued to be a problem for the T&G. I sat on the national co-ordinating committee, which was made up of all the regional organizers and chaired by Bill, and we drew up a national plan of action on campaigns. We launched the Link Up campaign to boost membership. The idea was that workers should link up with the T&G. Each region was asked to identify target areas where they could attract new members. This was the first time the regions had been told by central office to do this. The regions hated being told what to do. They preferred to do things on their own. Many regional secretaries didn't like Bill, either because of his style or his politics. We produced posters, leaflets and other publicity materials, all paid for by central office.

With the demise of the work done by men and the growth of the service industries and part-time jobs, we introduced a campaign called Full-Time Rights for Part-Time Workers and Permanent Rights for Temporary Workers. Around a third of the estimated 1,750,000 temporary workers were women, concentrated mainly in badly paid industries such as cleaning and catering; and around 96 per cent of the 5 million part-time workers were women. Temporary workers got a very bad deal. They had no right to a pension, maternity leave, holiday or sick pay.

Bill Morris led the campaign. This was a straight fight for a directive to give employment protection to part-time workers. When we ran a fair pay campaign, we provided advice to officers on how to negotiate pay deals, explaining that it was important to make sure that the lower grades were not neglected and therefore incentives should be on a flat rate, not on percentages.

The members of the committee agreed with me that we needed to publicize what we were doing. The union published a newspaper, called *The Record*, but it rarely featured women in its pages. So I discussed the idea with Frances O'Grady, who was responsible for equality issues in the research department. She was very keen and spoke to Bill about it. He agreed that we need a publication that reflected our concerns. And a few weeks later we launched a quarterly magazine called *Together*.

I spent much of my time as national organizer visiting workplaces around the country. I only ever visited somewhere if a local official invited me. It was not the done thing just to turn up unannounced. I would talk to the shop stewards about what the union could offer and give them leaflets and posters. Local officials then began to recruit members in small workplaces. In Wales, for example, officials tried to recruit employees in new electronic factories, while in Hull they ran a very successful equal pay campaign in fish factories.

As I mentioned earlier, I've always enjoyed visiting factories. You often get to see things being made that you have never thought much about. I remember visiting a factory in the Midlands that made wing-mirrors for cars. I had to try and look very interested and enthusiastic as a shop steward explained the various types.

We developed a recruitment programme with Sainsbury's. Most of its drivers and warehouse staff were union members, but not those on the shop floor. Sainsbury's agreed to let us visit to explain the work of the union. Many years before, Sainsbury's had signed an agreement to recognize both the T&G and USDAW, the shop workers' union. Paul Davies, the regional organizer in Liverpool, had done a fantastic job in recruiting women workers at Sainsbury's stores in Merseyside. The T&G decided to give him a national role, and I had to supervise him. Among other things, he visited Sainsbury's stores across London.

We ran a campaign called About Time, meaning 'it's about time you joined the union', targeting various trade groups in the regions and adapting our publicity material to them.

Yet, despite all these efforts, I felt that I was fighting a losing battle in trying to recruit new members. We might recruit thirty members in a small engineering company, but the factory down the road would close and we would lose three hundred members. It was obvious that the trade-union movement was never going to have the same clout it had in the 1970s, partly because the membership was smaller, partly because of demographics, and partly because more people were working in small companies. The more people in a workforce who don't have experience of trade unions, the less likely unions are to grow. One T&G officer said to me,

'When you go round a council estate and see different windows on a house and a little lantern hanging outside, you know someone has bought their house and turned into a Tory.' I agreed with him. Thatcher's policies had created a very different world from the one where the unions could call the shots.

The union has always got involved with health issues. For women, abortion is one of the most important. But, of course, it's also something that produces strong feelings among those who don't agree with it. When we ran a campaign about a woman's right to choose whether to have an abortion, and I sent leaflets out to each region, Mike Davey, the regional secretary in the Yorkshire region, who was a devout Catholic, simply ignored them. I felt that, whatever his own view was, he should let women make up their own mind about it.

'What do you think I should do?' I asked Bill.

'It's best to let it go,' he said. 'Don't fall out with people unnecessarily, Margaret.'

I took his advice, but it seemed wrong. While I respected Davey's views on abortion, I felt that he should also respect those who believed the opposite. But I knew that what Bill was saying was, 'If you want to get anywhere in the T&G, don't upset those people who have the power.' He didn't mean that you should never speak out, but rather that you shouldn't take on a fight you were never going to win. I was never going to win against Davey, as he, like all regional secretaries, had total control over any information sent out in his region.

One of the early tasks Bill gave me was to improve relations between the union and recruitment agencies. On one occasion we held a meeting and dinner at the Landmark Hotel on Marylebone Road with agencies from across Europe. In Britain there are several large agencies, such as Manpower, but hundreds of smaller ones. In continental

Europe, on the other hand, most of the agencies are very large. We were concerned that a proposed European directive giving temporary workers the same rights as permanent workers would be flouted by the smaller agencies. Later, the bad practice of some of these small agencies (commonly known as gangmasters) was exposed when twenty-three Chinese cockle-pickers died on the sands of Morecambe Bay in 2004. This led to the Gangmasters' Licensing Authority being established to oversee how they operated.

Bill was clever, imaginative and articulate. And he always encouraged me in my work. While I got on well with him and felt that he would do everything to put issues affecting women at the top of his agenda, I have to admit that I sometimes found him difficult. But I recognized that the role of general secretary was not an easy one. Bill had been given no training for it and had nowhere to turn for advice. He just had to get on with it. Although he could be very sharp with people, he didn't like conflict. I wondered if this was because he lacked self-confidence.

When I had to carry out a survey among staff to find out what their training needs were, I presented my results to Bill and he asked me to implement it. I told him I couldn't, as I didn't have the experience. The proposal sat on his desk and never saw the light of day. I was annoyed about this, as I had raised people's hopes about training and then nothing happened.

When the Labour Party asked me to speak about the national minimum wage at the annual conference in 1998, I said I would be happy to do this, but I would have to clear it with Bill first. I didn't think there would be a problem. However, I was wrong. Bill told me I couldn't do it. He said I needed to focus on my union work. This was because the national minimum wage was a touchy subject. The union was pushing for a higher level than the government was likely to accept. If I had spoken for the Labour Party, then

I would have had to take its line. I was annoyed and couldn't see why he wouldn't let me speak about an issue I knew a lot about and that was at the heart of the T&G's agenda.

In November I went to the T&G's residential centre in Eastbourne for a weekend conference for national officers. Because the centre was too small for the numbers expected, we hired a small theatre nearby. As general secretary, Bill stayed in a flat at the centre. On the Saturday morning he asked Ray Collins and myself to meet him there. We had hardly walked through the door when he launched into an attack on us both, accusing us of going behind his back and saying that he felt he couldn't trust us. He seemed to think we were plotting against him.

'You think you can work with Labour without me, don't you?' he said.

'What do you mean, Bill?' I replied.

'You wanted to speak at the Labour Party conference,' he shouted.

'Have you been dwelling on this all that time?'

'Don't be stupid, Bill,' said Ray.

Ray and I then left, both of us visibly shaken by Bill's outburst.

I was so upset by what Bill had said that I couldn't face the conference that afternoon. I told Ray that I was going to go for a walk instead. I need to clear my mind. Not far from the residential centre I bumped into Bill, who was chatting to someone in the street.

'Where are you going?' he said, breaking off his conversation.

'I'm going for a walk, actually.'

'I'll come with you.'

We walked towards the seafront in silence. As we neared the cliffs, he turned to me and said, 'I think we need to park that conversation. Not everyone's right all the time.'

This was as close as he could come to an apology. He knew he was in the wrong.

'OK, Bill,' I said, but I really felt that I wanted to thump him.

Bill didn't object to my work with the TUC. He felt respected by the TUC and at home in it. But he felt an outsider where the Labour Party was concerned.

I had been elected to the TUC executive council in 1988, and I was part of a delegation including Rodney Bickerstaffe, which went to see the employment minister in Whitehall. Many of the jobs in the public sector, for example in local government and the NHS, were being put out to compulsory competitive tendering, which was driving down pay because contracts were being given to the companies who would do the work most cheaply.

'Times are difficult for everyone and the government can't afford to increase public sector pay,' said the minister.

When he said this, Rodney went crimson. 'Well, why pay them anything at all?' he asked.

'I beg your pardon?' said the minister, looking shaken.

'Why don't you go out on to the streets, drag people in and tell them you're not going to pay them anything.'

'Sorry?'

'Your policies are keeping many people on low pay. That's wrong.'

I can't remember what the minister replied, but our efforts were in vain. As we thought, the government wasn't the slightest bit interested in those on low pay.

In 1994 the T&G left Transport House and moved to offices in Palace Street, a short distance from St James's Park. My office was on the seventh floor, and when I looked out of the window I could see trees in the gardens of Buckingham Palace. I had a beautiful walnut desk and cabinet that had belonged to Jack Jones. On the walls I put framed posters of some of the campaigns I had been involved in and the photos Ron Todd had given me, and I scattered mementoes from some of my trips abroad around the room.

The T&G employed a chauffeur to drive the general secretary around. He had the cheek of Old Nick. He was one of those people who have an answer for everything. At conferences he would often come to breakfast in our hotel, even though he wasn't staying there, pull up a chair and call across the dining room to one of us, 'All right now, love. Lovely last night, wasn't it?' implying that you might have been with him. It was very embarrassing.

One day, I was standing talking to someone in the outer secretary's office when the chauffeur walked past, swearing.

I said, 'You shouldn't swear. What if the general secretary hears you?'

'Fuck the general secretary,' he said.

I replied, 'Why don't you tell him to his face?'

'What do you mean?'

'Well, he's standing right behind you.'

He spun round to see a bemused Bill Morris staring at him. I had a job to keep a straight face. For once, he was lost for words.

Around this time I came to the end of my stint on the board of the Equal Opportunities Commission. I had served on it for seven years. The commission reflected a broad range of backgrounds. When I first joined, the chair was Baroness Beryl Platt, a Tory who had trained as an engineer and also been a local councillor in Norfolk. She always used to say, 'I always carry a spanner in my handbag.'

She was succeeded by Joanna Foster, who suggested we met the night before the board meetings for a meal at a hotel in Piccadilly, Manchester. It was quite formal, and I found it unnecessary. I've never been a fan of eating and discussing at the same time. When Joanna was chair, Valerie Amos was chief executive. But each of them behaved as though she had the opposite role: Valerie was always out and about attending meetings, while Joanna never left the office.

Kamlesh Bahl became chair in 1993, and I never got on with her. She was very divisive and behaved like a bully and made the staff unhappy. On one occasion she called Anne Gibson and myself into her office to remind us that if we were campaigning in the general election we had to remain neutral as commissioners.

I said, 'I've been campaigning in elections and working in a professional capacity for a long time. I think I know the difference.'

'Oh, I don't mean to offend you,' she said.

I said, 'I know which hat I'm wearing when I'm saying what.' I thought she had a cheek.

Diana Brittan, wife of (later Lord) Leon Brittan, became deputy chair for a time. She was very ladylike and brought a lot of valuable experience with her. She also had a mischievous sense of humour. When Leon was appointed to Europe and gave up his seat in Yorkshire, she said, 'Thank God we don't have to support that woman any more.' She meant Margaret Thatcher.

The commission was able to conduct formal investigations and had the legal powers to go into an organization and inspect documents. For example, I once conducted an investigation into the appointment of midwives by a health authority in Derbyshire. The commission would help someone take a case to an employment tribunal only if it was a case of note, in other words if it might set a precedent. One such case involved Dan Air, which, it transpired, refused to employ male cabin crew. They argued that it was well known that male cabin crew were gay and, because of this, might carry HIV, and therefore pose a health and safety risk to passengers. The real reason, of course, was that women accepted lower wages, so they were cheaper to employ. In the end, the airline had to make a public apology and afterwards it sent bouquets of flowers to all its cabin crew.

In another case, in 1986 Helen Marshall, who worked in a medical laboratory in Southampton, was forced to retire at the age of sixty-two. She took her case to the European Court and won. It found that the Southampton and South West Area Health Authority had been wrong to sack her since men were allowed to continue working until the age of sixty-five. Under European law, men and women must receive equal treatment. This case led to the equalisation of the retirement age of men and women—upwards, of course. While I can understand why Helen Marshall wanted to work on, women who do a job such as plucking chickens probably don't want to carry on working. If you're doing interesting work, then you might want to continue working, but if you are doing monotonous and unpleasant work then you probably don't.

The largest number of cases that came before us concerned pregnant women being dismissed from work. There were so many that we couldn't keep up with them. When I suggested at one of our board meetings that we launch a campaign to raise awareness of this, everyone agreed. It was very successful and was even featured on BBC Radio 4's *Woman's Hour*.

As far as I could see, the major problem for the Equal Opportunities Commission was that, on the one hand, it was run like the civil service, because it was accountable to government, which meant it was plodding and thorough, but, on the other hand, it was supposed to be imaginative and campaigning. The two things didn't sit well together.

I was now very involved in the international union scene and travelling regularly to different countries. In April 1994 I attended the International Confederation of Free Trade

Unions (ICFTU) women's conference in The Hague and in September a meeting of the International Chemical Energy and Mining Workers (ICEM) executive committee in Sofia. While I thought The Hague was a very pleasant and attractive city, Sofia was grim. Although ICEM had paid in advance for both the hotel and meals, the waiters wouldn't give you an extra bottle of wine unless you gave them money. I thought they had a bloody cheek.

In September 1995 I attended the Fourth World Conference on Women, organized by the Commission on the Status of Women, a committee of the UN, in Beijing. As this was the tenth anniversary of the founding of the commission it was a very important conference. I went as the chair of the TUC women's committee, representing all the female trade-union members in the UK, and travelled with Jo Morris, a TUC policy officer. As the conference was such a long way away and in such an interesting country, we decided to have a holiday on our way there.

So in late August we made our way through the crowds of holidaymakers at Heathrow and boarded a British Airways flight to Hong Kong. I had never travelled to the Far East, but friends who had been there all told me it was a fascinating part of the world. I knew very little about China except that it was vast, contained nearly a fifth of the world's population, and had been ruled by emperors until the revolution that turned it into a Communist country. Of course, like everyone else, I had sat watching the awful pictures on TV of the army shooting dead those protesting for democracy in Beijing's Tiananmen Square in 1989.

We spent two nights in Hong Kong. While we were there, on the second evening I celebrated my fifty-eighth birthday on a restaurant cruise boat with a bunch of Australians. We then caught a connecting flight to the city of Guillin in south-west China. A colleague at the T&G had been there and told me how nice it was. It was one of the friendliest cities

I'd ever been in. Several times when we were walking down a street we found ourselves joined by a locals who wanted to practise their English. I remember visiting a department store that seemed to have hardly anything in it. One morning, we took a boat trip up the Lei River, travelling through a landscape of what are known as 'the little pointed mountains'.

We then flew to Xi'an to visit the museum containing the terracotta army. We hired a young guide in Xi'an. He had an unpronounceable name, so he asked us to call him Tiger. I nicknamed him Tiger Lily after the character in the Rupert Bear books. He was hopeless, and had only got the job because his father ran a travel agency. I hadn't realized that the terracotta army consisted of so many figures. There were hundreds. What was amazing was that each one of them had a different expression on its face. When the young lad began telling us about the history of the figures, Jo ignored him and put on a pair of headphones to listen instead to an audio tour in English. He seemed hurt and I felt a bit sorry for him. Jo was laughing and said that as she wasn't coming back again she didn't care.

We arrived in Beijing five days before the conference began. We had been allocated our hotel before we left London. It was near a large stadium. By no means was it posh and most of the girls working there didn't seem to have a clue. When I looked out of the window the next morning I was amazed to see people doing tai chi in the hotel gardens. We spent the day walking along a section of the Great Wall and the next day wandering through the Forbidden City. With its pagodas, marble and pathways, it was very beautiful. I could easily imagine the emperor and his entourage riding through it.

Special buses had been organized from the delegates' hotels to the conference centre. It was a massive place, guarded by dozens of armed police. Students in T-shirts acted as stewards, telling everyone where to go. At conferences in the

UK and elsewhere, you always get people selling things. But there was no one doing this in Beijing. We were all given maps of the city written in Chinese and English. I had nightmares about losing mine, because if I needed to get a taxi I just pointed on the map to where I wanted to go and the driver knew what I meant.

At UN conferences there is the governments' agenda and a second agenda reflecting voluntary organizations. We were part of the second agenda. It took me some time to understand the schedule, as it was very complicated. I spoke at one of the secondary events, held in a large marquee. I gave an overview of some of the developments in women's rights in Britain. I made sure I didn't speak too quickly so that the interpreters could understand. At one conference I had attended an interpreter came out of her box and asked if a T&G member was speaking English, because he had such a strong cockney accent.

Hillary Clinton had been invited to attend, but had refused to come as a government representative because of China's human rights record. So she spoke at one of the secondary events instead, criticizing the Chinese government, which I thought was pretty inappropriate. I bet she would be more careful now. I hope she has learnt a bit about international relations since she has been US Secretary of State. It's not always as straightforward as you might hope, I guess.

We went on a day out with other union representatives visiting a nursery and a training centre for airline staff run by China Airways and Lufthansa. I think we were taken there because China Airways had a terrible reputation for safety and they wanted to show how they had now improved. We were invited to get on a half plane, used for training. All of a sudden, smoke started coming up out of the floor and lights began to flash. We didn't know if it was real. The next minute, several cabin crew members started running up and down the aisle, shouting at us in Chinese. We were ordered to place our heads between our legs. A young girl came and roughly shoved my head down. Jo and I were in hysterics. Then the noise and smoke stopped as suddenly as it had begun.

Afterwards Jo and I invited the international officer of the All China Federation of Trade Unions, who had organized the day out, to come back for a drink with us. As we chatted, he expressed his anger at the students who protested in Tiananmen Square, claiming that they had all gone abroad now. He said change had to happen slowly. What if China became like Yugoslavia, fragmented into different parts? I could understand his anxieties, as the former Yugoslavia was now a mess.

At the end of the conference, a thick document called the Platform for Action was produced, setting out what every country should sign up to in terms of the rights of women. This document is revisited and updated every year at the Commission on the Status of Women meetings at the UN in New York.

I sold my house in Thornton Heath in the summer of 1997 and bought a flat a few miles away in Beckenham. Because the flat wasn't ready in time for me to move into, I'd had my post diverted to my daughter Carol's house in Sanderstead. She drove over one morning to give me a hand with the move and brought me some post. One of the letters had Buckingham Palace written on it, and I assumed it was an invitation to a garden party or something. But I nearly fell through the floor when I read it. It said I was to receive an OBE. I rushed into the living room, waving the letter in the air. 'Carol! Guess what? I'm going to get the OBE.' Carol looked stunned. 'Mum, you deserve it,' she said, jumping up. When I read the letter a second time, I knew that the TUC had nominated me, because the Thornton Heath postcode was wrong. Whenever I received a letter from the TUC it always had the wrong postcode.

On 31 August I celebrated my sixtieth birthday and my OBE with my family and friends at a hotel in Letchworth, Hertfordshire. I actually turned sixty on 22 August, but decided to celebrate it a week or so later, so that everyone would be back from their holidays. But I remember that birthday for another reason. Early on the Sunday morning I woke up to the sound of my daughter Carol banging on the door. She told me Princess Diana had been killed in a car crash in Paris. Like everyone else, I was shocked by the news.

I went to Buckingham Place to receive my OBE on 13 November 1997. Carol, Stella and Jeffrey and their partners came as my guests. Carol's husband, Steven, my grandson Harry, who was two months old, and Ray Collins joined us later. The staff at the palace made me feel as if I was the only person who had ever received an OBE. They were lovely. And I was thrilled to meet the Queen, who gave me a warm smile as she pinned the medal on me. After the ceremony, we all went to the Four Seasons Hotel on Park Lane for lunch. It was a truly wonderful and memorable day.

That same year, I organized a series of trade-based conferences. The purpose was to encourage participation in the union and explore the issues in particular sectors. Bill and I came up with the idea as part of our presentation plan.

Organizing a conference requires a lot of attention to detail. You have to find a suitable venue, which isn't always easy; book speakers; identify the delegates (and make sure their expenses and loss of earnings are paid); produce a brochure and leaflets; arrange for photographers; and ensure that teas and lunches are provided. Bill asked Frank Doran, who had been MP for Aberdeen South until he lost his seat in the 1992 general election, to help me.

We held conferences on different themes. For example, in Leeds it was energy and in Birmingham manufacturing. Union officials, local MPs, business leaders and academics attended the conferences.

However, I have to confess that we came up with the idea for the conferences partly to boost my profile for when the election came up for deputy general secretary. We thought it would be a great achievement for a woman to become the first deputy general secretary of the T&G. And I'd be lying if I said that I didn't want to be at the top.

10. Peacocks and Feather Dusters

DURING MY SIX YEARS as T&G national organizer I served as president of the TUC. The presidency, which lasts for a year, is regarded as the most senior position in the trade-union movement. I'd actually been due to take it up at the end of the 1996 TUC congress, but after I returned from the UN conference in Beijing in September 1995 I was told that it had been brought forward a year because Tony Dubbins, the general secretary of the print workers' union, had decided to not to take up the appointment until the following year because his wife had recently died. I was only the third woman to serve as president; Marie Patterson and Ada Maddocks were the only other women to have held the position.

I took over the presidency from Leif Mills, general secretary of the banking, insurance and finance union, at the end of the TUC annual congress at Blackpool in September 1995. My year as president was incredibly hectic, as I still had my T&G work to do and I also had to attend ICEM meetings, but it was without doubt one of the most enjoyable and fascinating periods of my career. The TUC and I agreed on a list of engagements, which mostly fitted in with my particular interests, and I gave them a copy of my diary so that they knew what I was up to. I spent much of the time on the road, attending union conferences and special events and visiting universities. I usually gave a speech at least once a week, something that even someone as talkative as me didn't always find easy.

One of the main jobs of the president is to chair the general council and the executive council, which meet at Congress House in Great Russell Street. The general council is made up of general secretaries from the unions and also long-serving officials. Every union with over 100,000 members has a right to a seat on it. Larger unions have more seats than smaller ones. The T&G had three seats. Six seats were reserved for women. Unions with fewer than 100,000 members had to hold elections for the remaining eight seats. In the late 1980s, the rules had changed and four additional seats were given to women from smaller unions. The executive council, which was a sub-committee of the general council, was made up of the general secretaries of the big unions and other senior officials, and it looked at issues in more detail and then made recommendations to the general council, which, in most cases, endorsed them.

One of my first official engagements was at an anti-racism rally in Manchester, where I led a crowd of several hundred people through the city centre, walking alongside Neville Lawrence—the father of black teenager Stephen Lawrence who had been stabbed to death by a group of white youths while waiting for a bus in south-east London—and the TUC general secretary, John Monks. When we arrived in St Peter's Square, where a stage had been erected outside the town hall, Neville Lawrence made a speech. John and I sat alongside him. But a rowdy group of Trots at the front of the crowd began shouting to try and drown him out. He kept stopping and saying slowly, 'My son has been murdered.' But they didn't take any notice and shouted even louder. I felt like jumping down off the stage and smacking each one of the louts in the face. It was heart-breaking to see a man still grieving for his son having to endure this kind of appalling behaviour. When a local radio reporter interviewed me afterwards, I didn't mince my words.

In February 1996, I flew to Belfast with John Monks to take part in a peace rally. Earlier that month, a massive bomb had exploded at Canary Wharf, ending the IRA ceasefire that had been in place since August 1994. Several thousand people turned out for the rally. I was supposed to make a speech standing on the back of a lorry in front of City Hall.

But the lorry didn't arrive on time, so I had to make the speech standing on the ground, which meant no one could see me. It was very frustrating, but I suppose, even though it was a very serious event, it also must have looked comical.

My diary was packed, and I was having a trouble fitting in all the engagements. One weekend I made a brief visit to the USDAW conference in Blackpool in a chauffeur-driven car provided by John Monks. After I had made my speech that evening, I became worried that I was going to struggle to be on time for a lifelong learning conference I was due to open at Congress House early in the morning.

We left the hotel at the crack of dawn. The driver gave me a pillow and I put the front seat right back and nodded off. But we got stuck in heavy traffic on the M6 and I arrived at the conference forty-five minutes late. When I walked in, everyone sitting there turned to look at me as if to say, 'Where have you been?' John Monks whispered to me, 'You've now become a friend of the M6.'

In June, I flew to Rome to take part in an EU meeting between governments, employers and unions. I stayed in a beautiful hotel overlooking the hills of Rome and went for dinner one evening at a medieval palace. I'd only been back in London a few days when I was packing my suitcase again and, this time, boarding the Eurostar train at Waterloo for an ICFTU conference in Brussels.

Every July, a couple of thousand trade-union members and locals gather in the village of Tolpuddle in the Dorset countryside for a march and festival to celebrate the six farm workers who became known as the Tolpuddle Martyrs and were, in many ways, the founders of the trade-union movement in England. In the early 1830s, when the wages of farm labourers were being reduced, they started the Friendly Society of Agricultural Labourers, insisting on a minimum wage of ten shillings a week. The men were arrested for unlawful assembly and brought for trial at the Dorchester

Assizes. They were sentenced to seven years in a penal colony in New South Wales, Australia. The men were hailed as heroes for standing up for the right of workers to a just wage and people took to the streets to protest over their sentences. Union members took care of their families while they were away. In 1836 the government caved in to public pressure and revoked the sentences; the men were allowed back to England after serving just three years in the colony. In 1934, to commemorate the centenary of the trial, the TUC built six cottages and founded the Tolpuddle Martyrs Museum.

The organizers of the day had decided that, as the TUC president that year was a woman, there would be an all-female platform, consisting of myself; Angela Billingham, MEP for Northamptonshire and Blaby; Jean Corston, MP for Bristol East; Sue Longley, from the international food workers' union; and Pauline Green, MEP for London North. We were sitting in a marquee, waiting to be called when a local official wandered over to us and said, 'Have you worked out what you are going to say?'

'How do you mean?' I asked.

'Well, we don't want you all saying the same thing.'

I couldn't believe what I was hearing. We were some of the most senior union and political figures in the country and he seemed to think that because we were women we didn't know how to make a speech. I looked at Shirley, Bill Morris' secretary, and I could see she was fuming. She then stood up and walked out. Afterwards, she said to me, 'If I had stayed there, I would have hit him.' The rest of us thought it was hilarious and decided the man was an idiot.

As TUC president, I chaired the TUC–Labour Party contact group, although it didn't officially exist. It consisted of TUC senior officials and the Labour shadow cabinet, who included Tony Blair, Gordon Brown, Patricia Hewitt, Jack Straw and John Prescott. We met informally at Congress House to exchange views about important issues. For example, when David Blunkett's shadow education department produced a paper on the future of education and training we had a discussion about it, as the unions were very influential over training in the workplace.

One issue about which I wanted to raise more awareness during my year as president was the low pay of part-time workers. I'd worked part-time when I was bringing up the kids and my mum had also worked part-time when I was growing up. My first speech at a TUC conference, in 1985, had been about rights for part-time workers. When I spoke about this at the 1995 conference *The Independent* ran a story entitled 'The Twilight World of "New Workhouses"'. There were an estimated six million people working part-time.

Following the introduction of compulsory competitive tendering for council services and then, in 1993, the abolition of wages councils, the pay of part-timers—the majority of whom were women—had been hit hard. Many were employed in businesses, such as private nursing homes and sweatshops, that were little more than modern-day workhouses, earning as little as £1.50 an hour.

Under Tory policies, the gap between those with full-time jobs and those with part-time jobs was widening. For some, part-time work is an attractive option, but for others it is the only way to combine the need to earn an income with the demands of family life. A growing number of people were simply unable to find full-time work. Nearly a million people were forced to juggle two or more jobs in order to earn a living.

I always felt that the union movement should be the natural home for these workers. But many of them were terrified to speak out and join a union for fear of the sack.

The British trade-union movement is well regarded around the world, partly because we have only one main union body, the TUC. In France, for example, there are three such bodies.

Just as I was about to leave the office one day I received a phone call from Mike Walsh at the international department of the TUC to say they had received a request for a representative to address the Fijian TUC congress. I thought to myself, well, I can't say no to this.

'What we need to do is organize a programme,' he said, adding that if I flew via the west coast of the United States he could arrange for me to meet the American Federation of Labor in San Francisco before flying on to Fiji via New Zealand.

I was so excited that I ran down the corridor and burst into Ray's office.

'Guess what?'

'What?'

'The TUC's just asked me to go to Fiji.'

'Blimey.'

'It would be great if you could came as well.'

'Wouldn't it.' He looked thoughtful and then grinned, 'Leave it with me.'

Ray was very cross with Bill Morris. Bill had promised him first choice for which weeks to be on holiday in the summer. But Bill booked his holiday without telling Ray. He knew Ray was still unhappy about this. So he asked Bill if he could accompany me to Fiji. He agreed, as Ray guessed he would.

The T&G paid for Ray and the TUC paid for me. The trip would be for nine days. We flew first to San Francisco, where we met the president of the California Labor Federation at a swish office block in the centre of the city. He must have been in his eighties. He told us that he had worked for Roosevelt and had known many political figures in the US. He took us to lunch at an Italian restaurant around the corner. It was very old-fashioned: all wood with lace curtains.

The owner had what my dad use to call patent leather hair and reminded me of George Raft. Over a couple of bottles of wine and excellent pasta, he told us stories about his early days in the union. When Ray and I left we were in hysterics because we couldn't get over how ancient the president looked.

I loved San Francisco. Ray and I walked across the Golden Gate Bridge and took a tram up one of the many hills in the city. I remember in the middle of the tram was a man whose job it was to apply the brake. Gazing out to the sea, we could see Alcatraz, the famous prison, in the distance.

We then flew to Hawaii, where we changed planes and flew on to Fiji. Because the main airport in Fiji was at one side of the island and Suva, the capital, was at the other, we had to take a small plane to Suva. Before we got on we had to be weighed with our luggage.

When Ray settled into his seat, his face turned ashen. The windows weren't the usual small ones that most planes have. They were huge. Ray can't stand heights. When the plane set off down the small runway, he covered his head with a newspaper and kept saying, 'I can't look, Margaret! I can't look.'

I have to admit that it was a scary flight. We flew low over mountains and wooded valleys, and the windows made you feel very exposed.

As soon as I stepped off the plane at Suva's tiny airport, I could feel the humid heat rising up. It was overpowering. We were met by representatives of the TUC and the teaching and nursing unions, and then taken by taxi to our hotel, set behind large palm trees. My room overlooked the ocean. The view was spectacular. We were both shattered and decided we needed to sleep for a few hours.

That evening, we attended a reception at a community hall. When I walked in, a woman came up to me and placed a ring of flowers around my neck, and immediately a swarm of small flies appeared. I took my seat at a table and then a man appeared at my side, holding a plastic washing-up bowl with what looked like washing-up water in it. It was Kava, the national drink, which is made from some plant or other and is narcotic. He dipped a ladle in it and offered it to me. I didn't really want it, as it looked and smelled disgusting, but I thought it would appear rude if I refused, so I took a sip, and it tasted as bad as it looked, but I did my best to smile. 'Thank you.' Ray had read that the drink helped to clear your mind, so he eagerly took several sips of it. Later on, when we were introduced to members of the government, he could hardly speak, as his mouth had gone numb.

We had a meeting with Fiji's MPs, most of whom turned out to be Indian. One of the guides told me that the Indians in Fiji make up the professional classes. He explained that the British had brought Indian workers over to build roads on the island. When we met the British ambassador, he told us there had been a coup a couple of years before because there was anger that all the senior positions in the civil service and government were held by Indians. Many Indians emigrated after the coup, which led to the Fijian government's tax revenue falling dramatically.

I gave a talk about the need for international trade and solidarity at a modern community centre and afterwards was interviewed by Radio Fiji. The next day, when we were driving to a picnic with some representatives of the teachers' union and their families, we stopped at a roadside pizza takeaway.

The man behind the counter looked at me and grinned, 'I know you.'

'Really,' I replied.

'Yes, I heard you on the radio.'

I felt like some international celebrity.

We then flew to Auckland in New Zealand, where we met some senior union officials. Ray flew to another island to meet friends. I couldn't face another flight, so I stayed in Auckland, which is a tiny city and very dull. I went out for dinner with the president of one of the unions and the next night went to dinner with some women who worked for the banking union.

The trip to Fiji was hugely enjoyable and lots of fun. But there were other fun moments during the year. I remember finding it hilarious that a man I marched with on a May Day rally in Newcastle-upon-Tyne, for some reason, referred to himself as 'Larch of the Trees'. It was a long way from the big May Day rallies that had been held by the miners and shipbuilders. I also remember standing in a field at a T&G Midlands region family fun day and watching members of the Red Devils parachute team land. I then heard one of them call out, 'Is Margaret Prosser there?' He ran over to me and presented me with a baton to congratulate me on being TUC president. And after I spoke at the International Association of Women Police Officers conference, I was presented with a truncheon. When I went to the Co-operative movement conference in Harrogate, I found it very amusing to see that one of the woman sitting on the platform was wearing a huge hat. It felt like a throwback to the 1950s when it would have been unthinkable for a woman to appear at this kind of event without a hat on.

In some ways, despite all the various legislation to give women the same opportunities as men, it sometimes felt that we were still in the 1930s. When I attended the annual CBI dinner at the Grosvenor Hotel in Park Lane I don't remember seeing any women sitting at the tables. All I can remember is a sea of men in black suits. As an aside, a few years later Digby Jones, the head of the CBI, once gave evidence to the Low Pay Commission I was sitting on. He had such an air of self-importance about him. Afterwards, John Cridland, who later went on to become head of the CBI, said to me, 'You're lucky. You only have to put up with him once a year.'

My year as president came to a close at the end of the annual congress in Blackpool in September 1996. I travelled up on the Wednesday. As president, I had a suite at the Pembroke Hotel. My son and daughters and their partners and children came up on the Saturday and the TUC paid for them to stay in the hotel with me.

As president I had to chair the congress, something I was really looking forward to. There were two meetings early each morning. The first was in the hotel with Brendan Barber, the deputy general secretary, Jimmy Knapp, the vice-president, and some policy officials. The purpose of this was to run through the day's agenda. Sometimes things would have happened overnight which I might not know about, like a union changing its mind or agreement being reached on a difficult issue.

After breakfast we would then go to the conference centre for a meeting of the general council. This was usually very brief. We would agree what position we might be taking on various issues and who would be speaking in the debates. I was given a running sheet, which gave chapter and verse for everything I had to do. The reason it was so detailed was because in the past some presidents were either less able than others, or through a liking for the high life and too much to drink, didn't pay enough attention to what went on in the hall.

I had to attend numerous lunchtime and evening receptions put on throughout the week by different unions. Ray Collins was always at my side to make sure I didn't get collared for too long so we could move on to the next one. The driver provided by the TUC took us from hotel to hotel. This was when Ray and I became known as 'Victoria and Albert'. I also had to tour the exhibition stands and have a chat with the members on them. On the Sunday morning I helped lead the pensioners' rally, which Jack Jones had organized for many years. In the evening, I hosted the T&G/GMB reception, which was always attended by senior union and Labour Party figures.

On Tuesday, before the president's dinner or, as it is sometimes called, the fraternal delegates' dinner, I went to John Monks' hotel suite to have a drink with him and Tony Blair. When I came out of the lift I saw Brendan Barber pacing up and down the corridor.

'I don't think you should go in there,' he said.

'Why?'

'Tony and John are having a row.'

I could hear shouting. 'What about?'

'This David Blunkett story.'

That morning, a story had appeared in the papers claiming that David Blunkett had suggested changing employment law. John Monks wanted to know why any changes hadn't first been discussed with the TUC. It seemed that Labour considered the trade-union movement dead and buried. Tony felt he could win the next election without the unions.

Tony and John then came out of the room, both looking angry. Behind them I saw a stony-faced Alistair Campbell, who was then still a journalist but was also helping Tony with his media campaign for the general election, and John Healy, the TUC communications officer, looking very awkward. I knew that the reason John Monks was so angry was because he, like some other senior union leaders, was trying hard to modernize the trade-union movement and bring it more in line with Labour's policies, and he was frustrated with Tony for not understanding that this all took time.

'Okay? Are we ready?' I said brightly, thinking, 'What on earth is going on?'

As we walked down the corridor Tony turned round and shouted, 'I don't care what you say, Ali, just fucking get it right.'

We all got into the lift. No one spoke. Tony and John stared at the floor. I knew the press were hanging around downstairs in the lobby, so I said, 'OK, you two. Smile.' They both looked at me as if I was barking mad.

When the doors opened, a dozen journalists and photographers surrounded us. We all flashed a smile, giving no hint of what had just happened, and strode past them.

I sat next to Tony at the top table during the dinner in the hotel ballroom that evening. I didn't know him that well at this point, but I found him easy to chat to. He seemed to have cheered up since the incident with John. In his speech, he spoke about Labour returning to power and the need for change. I can't remember exactly what I said in my speech, but I know I mentioned the word 'socialism', which made everyone in the hall laugh, as they thought Tony had forgotten it.

I thoroughly enjoyed chairing the conference. It gave me a real buzz. On the opening morning, a delegate made a joke about football at the end of his speech. As he walked away from the rostrum, I said, 'Can I just advise congress that's the first and last joke we are going to hear about football this week.' I was fed up with listening to men making football jokes at conferences. John Monks, who is a Manchester United fan, was astonished when I said this. At his retirement dinner a few years later, he told Sir Alec Ferguson what I had said. Ferguson said to me that football was a passion and implied I just didn't understand it. I did understand it, but I thought some men made too much of what is, after all, only a game.

Sitting on the platform alongside me were John Monks, Brendan Barber, whose job was to guide me, David Lea, the assistant general secretary, and Jimmy Knapp. The most senior members of the general council sat in the front rows, while the other members sat in a row behind me. On the table in front of me was what was known as the president's bell, which had my name engraved on it. There were also some peacock's feathers, provided by the TUC women's committee, because, as is often said, 'today's peacock is tomorrow's feather duster'. A lot of union leaders think they are peacocks, something I was reminded of when attending the receptions that week.

Most of the debates that year were about what kind of legislation we wanted a Labour government to support. Rodney Bickerstaffe made a rousing speech, arguing for a minimum wage of £4.26 an hour. He had been campaigning for a national minimum wage for years. A number of unions, including the T&G, took a long time to agree to this, insisting that collective bargaining was the best way forward. They saw legal measures as interference and undermining their role.

John Edmonds of the GMB made some sarcastic remarks in his speech. He was an Oxford scholar and saw himself as a bit above everyone else.

Arthur Scargill proposed a motion demanding non-compliance with the Tory anti-union laws, but he was defeated. His day had long gone. Many speakers referred to the plight of the Liverpool dockers, who had come to the conference in force, handing out leaflets and stickers and attending fringe meetings. Their dispute was, in fact, illegal. No ballot had been taken. They just walked off the job. So any official show of support was pretty difficult. The dockers were T&G members and it was very touchy for us, as official support for an illegal stoppage could result in the union being heavily fined and charged for the company's losses.

Resolutions were passed unanimously in favour of the RMT guards in their dispute over natural breaks and past productivity payments, and the Magnet kitchen workers, who were sacked after taking legally balloted strike action over a pay and conditions dispute. Some speakers criticized the greed of the privatized utilities, others called for the renationalization of the railways and an end to the government's Private Finance Initiative (PFI). Congress also backed a general council statement which, in effect, adopted the New Labour strategy.

It's interesting now to look at what's happened since then. Trains no longer always have guards on them and the PFI is discredited in the eyes of economists and most politicians. Most of our utilities are in foreign hands, with the CEOs paying themselves massive salaries.

The high point for me at the congress was my presidential speech. I had met up with Frances O'Grady, who was then a communications officer with the TUC and had been my researcher at the T&G, to discuss with her what I wanted to say. She then went away and wrote the speech. I knew she would strike the right note, and she did. Although I was used to giving speeches they tended to be quite brief. The president's speech at congress traditionally lasts about fifteen minutes, which, I was aware, is quite a long time to hold the attention of an audience.

When you begin a speech, if you don't hook your audience straight away, they are likely to lose interest. So I told a story about attending a stakeholders' conference at Sheffield University a few weeks before. A woman sitting next to me had said she was disappointed that there were so few trade unionists present, especially senior ones. 'Well, the president of the TUC is senior,' I replied. She said, 'Oh, I'm sorry. Is he here?' I was relieved when that got a laugh around the conference hall.

I then went on to attack Tory policies, ridiculing all the 'charters' that had been produced while many people in Britain, especially the young and women, were not paid a fair wage or had no work at all, and while the gap between rich and poor was worse today than at any time since the Second World War. I pointed out that two-thirds of mothers who wanted to work were unable to because of the lack of decent childcare.

But I didn't want my speech to be all doom and gloom. I wanted to give the delegates hope in a better future and something positive to take back to their workplaces and communities. I cited South Africa as an example of what real change looks like, and mentioned the emotional scenes I had witnessed a few months before when I stood in the crowd outside South Africa House in Trafalgar Square, listening to President Nelson Mandela talk of hope and a new future. The trade-union movement had to have this same sort of hope, I said.

On the final day of the conference John Monks read out a rap poem written by Bob Purkiss, the race officer for the T&G. It was to thank me for chairing the Congress and to acknowledge that I would be leaving the TUC and joining the Labour Party national executive committee (NEC) as treasurer.

> It must be lonely sat out there
> Controlling, guiding, as the chair,
> A sea of faces everywhere,
> Some nice, some kind, some not all there.
> Your sense of humour every day
> Helped delegates to find their way.
> I even heard one of them say,
> 'Elect for life; make her stay.'
> We'll miss you, Marg, at the TUC
> Your sense of fairness and equality
> Will help us where you're going to be.
> But tell 'em, Marg, nowt for free.

At the end of it, everyone in the hall burst into applause.

The T&G had two seats on the Labour NEC. One was held by Danny Duffy, who was due to come off it at the end of the Labour Party conference. The treasurer, who was with the GMB union, was also due to retire. The T&G had to lose one of its three seats on the TUC general council, because its membership had declined. So it was agreed that I would step down from the TUC general council and be put forward to be treasurer of the Labour Party. I was quite happy sitting on the TUC council, and felt I had made my name on it, but I could see the logic in the decision. I was also chairing the women's committee. Bill Morris persuaded the major unions to agree to vote for me to be the treasurer.

Party conferences were held in seaside resorts because the hotels were reasonably priced and tended to be on or just off the promenade, which meant it was easy to find everyone. Also, you could always find a cheap bed-and-breakfast. We once had a TUC conference in Glasgow but it didn't work well. The conference was held in a conference centre on the banks of the river Clyde, but the delegates were scattered in hotels across the city, which meant they had to travel backwards and forwards by bus or taxi.

Blackpool could claim to be the capital of party conferences. It's hosted dozens of them over the years. Its only attraction seems to be that the streets running off the promenade are packed with cheap hotels and B&Bs, which means that delegates have more money left for beer. I've lost count of the number of times I've walked along the promenade on my way to the Winter Gardens, with the trams clanking past and the wind from the Irish Sea nearly blowing me off my feet.

But I've never liked Blackpool. The Winter Gardens were a real dump and often smelled of last night's beer. They were built for shows and events and were quite glitzy. But they are unsuitable for conferences. The ballroom is uncomfortable and has poor acoustics, and the researchers have nowhere to sit and do their work. One year at the T&G biennial conference, delegates sat with their umbrellas up because rain was coming through the roof. Another proper centre was built, but it was too small for most of the national conferences, and then there was apparently a row between Blackpool Council and the new centre, and none of our people used it.

There is nowhere in Blackpool to get a decent meal or a glass of wine. When I once stayed in the presidential suite at a modern hotel, I asked the receptionist if I could have a bar in my room so that I could entertain guests.

'Of course. I'll arrange that for you when you are out.'

When I returned I couldn't believe my eyes. The 'bar' was a white kitchen fridge stuck on top of a dressing table. I went down to reception and complained. But the receptionist couldn't see what was wrong with it. I had to see the funny side, even though the fridge hummed and buzzed all night.

When I attended the GPMU women's conference, I stayed at the Norbreck Castle Hotel, a huge, grim place that sits on a hill. It looks like something out of Stalag 17. I had to push my way through thirteen sets of doors to reach my room. I said to another delegate, 'They should issue you with a pair of roller skates.'

Despite the cheap B&Bs, few delegates liked Blackpool. So in the end all the main parties and the TUC agreed not to return until the council did something about the Winter Gardens—but they still haven't.

The week after the TUC conference I was back in Blackpool again, this time for the Labour Party conference— as I was no longer TUC president, I had to queue in the rain like everyone else to get in to the Winter Gardens.

11. Piggy in the Middle

I'M SOMEONE WHO HAS NEVER been that great at maths and figures, although I've always been able to add up. I can still remember how I struggled with things such as percentages and fractions when I was at school. At primary school I used to cry because I couldn't understand what the teacher was talking about. But life is strange. In October 1996, shortly after the TUC Congress, I found myself elected treasurer of the Labour Party and therefore a member of the NEC. This wasn't my first national post in the party. I'd served for four years on the committee that organized the annual conference. Being on the NEC not only provided me with a ringside seat to watch the massive political changes that Tony Blair and New Labour were to usher in, but also landed me smack bang in the middle of a controversy over donors and party funding.

By now there was a very different political mood in Britain from when Thatcher was in power. It was clear that after seventeen years the Conservative Party was washed up. Scandals, such as that over cash for questions involving Neil Hamilton and others, and the jailing of Jonathan Aitken for perjury and perverting the course of justice, had shattered the Tories' image of being a party of family values. When John Major announced in March 1997 that there would be a general election, he said, as you would expect, that the Conservatives would win it. But when I asked taxi drivers, shopkeepers and other people I met if they were going to vote Conservative, not one person said yes. To me, it was clear that it was Tony Blair, fresh, charismatic and a family man, who appealed to the British public, not John Major.

Once you start preparing for an election it's like a well-oiled machine. Everyone in a political party and the affiliated trade unions knows what they have to do. Members take to the streets on rainy afternoons, delivering leaflets or knocking on doors, and union officers are stood down from their day-to-day jobs. Some pick up MPs at the crack of dawn and drive them around the country.

A number of trade unions launched a women's programme before the election and a group of us, including Harriet Harman, travelled to different parts of the country to talk about how Labour intended to give women a greater say in policies. Wearing our red rosettes, we visited shopping centres, schools and community groups. It was very tiring. We would meet at Euston station at 7.00 a.m. and often wouldn't arrive back in London until 9.00 p.m. But it was very exciting because we knew that Labour was going to get elected. People always gave us a warm welcome and seemed pleased that we had taken the trouble to travel all the way from London.

Of course, election campaigns cost money. Venues have to be found and booked, leaflets and posters printed, adverts taken out in newspapers, and coaches and, on occasion, even trains and helicopters hired. And temporary staff have to be recruited to help with all the admin and donkey work. Tony said that he wasn't going to lose the 1997 election simply because he didn't have enough money, so I knew I had to keep a close eye on things. I used to meet twice a week with David Pitt-Watson, the finance director, and go through exactly what money had been spent and what money had come in.

I will never forget the night of the 1 May 1997 election. I sat with a group of regional secretaries and national officials from the T&G in a room Bill had hired at the Westminster Hotel. He had also laid on food and drinks. We huddled around the TV, watching the results come in from across the country and cheering as Labour won yet another seat. Labour won by a landslide, taking 419 seats. It was incredible.

I was a member of the Employment Appeals Tribunal at that time, and someone there organized a sweepstake and each of us paid a fiver to guess the result of the election and the kind of majority Labour would get. I won five hundred quid. When I told Bill, who was also a member of the tribunal, he said, 'Five pound of that is mine.' I replied, 'Not now it's not.'

Tony Blair wrote to party activists to thank them for all their hard work. At the end of the letter he sent to me, he had written in own handwriting 'Thank you for all you have done and are doing for us. It is deeply appreciated. Love, Tony.' I had first met him in 1992 when I sat on the One Member One Vote committee, set up by John Smith to break the block vote of the unions. Bill Morris had intended to go but Ray had persuaded him not to, explaining that if he went on he would have to stand by decisions he might not like, whereas if I went on it, I could be blamed and Bill's hands would be clean. That's the role of a deputy.

A few weeks after the election, I went to Number Ten for the first time. Sally Morgan and Jon Cruddas, who both now held senior positions there, had asked to discuss their salaries. They were looking for an increase because their jobs had changed, as they were now serving the prime minister. Number Ten was much bigger than I'd imagined. From the outside it doesn't look that big. But when you go inside you realize it goes back a long way. It had a beautiful sweeping staircase with photos of former prime ministers on the wall. The rooms had very high ceilings and contained pale silk sofas and chandeliers. There were lots of beautiful clocks everywhere. I was surprised how small Tony's office was. It was very ordinary, and just had a desk and a small sofa in it. After listening to Sally and John, I agreed to recommend to Tom Sawyer, the Labour Party general secretary, that he put them up a couple of grades. It only seemed fair, as they were now doing jobs that would be more high-profile and pressured.

It wasn't long before many union leaders were publicly expressing disappointment about New Labour, feeling it pandered too much to *Daily Mail* readers and the City. There is some truth in this, but Tony had understood that unless he won over *Daily Mail* readers and the City, Labour would never be elected. He knew that if Labour was to win, then it had to gain seats in the south of England. And you will never win the seats in the south if you are only talking about poverty and people who don't have anything because, generally speaking, many people in the south are comfortably off.

The Labour Party and the trade-union movement have, of course, always been closely bound together. Margaret Thatcher's attempts to break the trade unions were also an attempt to cut off funding to the Labour Party, which has traditionally relied heavily on the contributions of union members. In the run-up to the election there had been a determination by Tony Blair, Peter Mandelson and others to show to the voters that the party was not the old party of the unions. It was New Labour.

New Labour wanted the unions' money but didn't want to be seen in public with them. The unions were seen as a bit like an embarrassing uncle. In order to distance itself from the unions New Labour even became hostile. Many trade-union leaders weren't happy with this, and said so when they spoke to senior Labour MPs at the TUC Congress.

In those early days of the new Labour government, some union leaders thought that a Labour government would repeal some of the union legislation Margaret Thatcher had introduced, such as the rules union members had to abide by before a strike, 'check off' and electing a new general secretary every five years.

However, secretly, lots of union members didn't want these laws changed. For example, having a ballot before a strike gave a union bargaining power. If the management knew that, say, 75 per cent of the workforce was prepared to go out on strike, then they would sit up and take notice and a deal could be done without a strike. And the unpredictability of lightning strikes was a nightmare for unions, as they had to pay strikers. Electing a new union general secretary every five years meant that a complete duffer wouldn't be able to stay in office for a long time.

When Tony had arrived at the TUC conference in Blackpool in 1995 Bill Morris was standing outside the Winter Gardens waiting to greet him. As Tony got out of his car and walked towards the building, Bill extended his hand. But Tony walked straight past and never even looked at him. When I spoke to Bill afterwards he was very upset and felt Tony had been rude.

'I can understand that you're upset, Bill, but we have to understand the long-term game here,' I said.

I could see that the reason Tony had ignored Bill was not out of rudeness, but because he was very conscious of wanting to create a new image for the party. He didn't want a photo of him and Bill shaking hands to appear in the next day's papers. If this had happened, then the press would have said, 'See, it's the same old Labour Party.' It was very hard but somehow necessary.

As a senior trade-unionist and also a member of the NEC, I felt like piggy in the middle. I knew that some other T&G officials thought that I had 'gone native', although no one said this to my face. They couldn't understand New Labour's policies. I argued New Labour's corner, but I could see that Tony's attitude was upsetting people. I thought it was unnecessary and that he didn't have to go that far. While I believed that Labour had to appeal to a much wider section of the British public than it had previously done, I still had some qualms about the way it was seeking to distance itself from the unions. I could see that Tony was going to need the unions in the end. They provided the ballast for the party. The constituencies could be very flaky.

The gap that was opening up between Labour and the unions concerned me. After an NEC meeting I said to Tony,

'You ought to ease up on John Monks. He's trying his best to find a way forward.'

'I hear what you say, Margaret,' he said.

'The unions are trying to modernize, you know,' I said. There were many of us in the union movement who were trying to make trade unions more democratic and inclusive.

Tony just smiled. I knew he wasn't convinced. He was impatient with the unions and wanted them to come round to his way of thinking. He couldn't understand that this all took time.

Tony was not the only political leader wary of the unions. When I flew to Pittsburgh in the US in 1997, a couple of weeks before the Labour Party conference, to address the annual conference of the American Federation of Labor and Congress of Industrial Organizations, I discovered that it wasn't only Tony who was distancing himself from the unions. Bill Clinton was as well. I was there as the British TUC delegate. I was sitting on the platform in front of an audience of several hundred union members and was due to speak after Bill Clinton. He made a strong speech, insisting that international trade was vital to the US economy. This wasn't the message the federation wanted to hear. After he finished, instead of going to shake the hands of the union leaders sitting in the front row, as expected, he leapt off the side of the stage and walked away with his minders. He did this because one of the leaders was involved in a financial scandal and he wanted to steer clear of any publicity that might reflect badly on him. When I spoke to the union leaders afterwards they were miffed at both Clinton's speech and the way he ignored them. I said, 'Well, Tony Blair's being doing this for years in the Labour Party.' Clinton was quite a pussycat in comparison.

The fact is that Tony never had a feel for the democratic process of trade unions. He always said, 'Who does the executive council of the trade-union movement speak for?

Does it speak for the members?' He was right. It didn't really speak for the members. Most of the time it only spoke for those who had a particular political agenda.

One of the reasons that the representative system at the T&G didn't work well was because we had far too many people who had lost their jobs in the 1980s but had remained as industrial representatives, even though they were no longer working in the industry. The union didn't employ them, but they were reliant upon the expenses they got paid. This was completely at odds with the system established by Ernest Bevin when he set up the union in 1922. It provided for a separation of power between the industrial representatives, regional representatives and the general secretary.

But another reason most union executive committees were not very representative was because, in many jobs, it was difficult to get time off to attend meetings. For example, on the T&G executive we had three dockers, one representing the dockers and two representing their regions. There was no one representing part-time workers. I thought a Labour government could have made it easier for workers to get time off to attend union meetings.

It's not hard to see why the trade-union leadership was never really turned on by Tony. The general secretaries thought after years of being cold-shouldered by Margaret Thatcher and, to a certain extent, John Major, that when Labour got back in power they would be brought back into the heart of decision-making. But, of course, this wasn't how Tony saw it.

When there was a fuel strike, Tony realized that he needed the unions. The strike, which was started by lorry-owners and logistics people, caused panic, as the pumps at petrol stations started to run dry. People were very worried that they wouldn't be able to get to work or wherever they needed to go. The oil refinery shop stewards then got caught up in it. The union convenor was on holiday at the time. Had he been there he would have probably seen the danger the strike posed to the economy and done something to prevent it happening.

Tony and even Gordon Brown didn't seem to know what to do. It was Andy Smith, the chair of the T&G, and a retired BP oil tanker driver, who went to Grangemouth oil refinery and managed to persuade the shop stewards to end the strike.

Around the time I joined the NEC, Labour had begun to think about a new system of policy-making, outlined in a document called Party in Power.

Under the old system the NEC would ask the unions to put forward resolutions for the annual conference. These would be published in a big book and then in May or June amendments would be invited. On the Saturday at the conference we would meet to bring together all the resolutions about particular topics. We would then discuss who was going to move the resolution and who was going to second it. It was a bit like bartering in the Middle Ages. But this system led to some bizarre resolutions. I remember Ray Collins once saying, 'In five minutes flat we had a resolution on the table to abolish the monarchy.' No one gave a toss about any of these resolutions.

The aim of the changes proposed was to reduce the policy-making role of the annual conference, where trade-union members cast 50 per cent of the votes. In the past, this had led to embarrassing situations when the Labour leadership had not been in tune with other sections of the party. The document changed the rules to ensure that resolutions didn't happen simply by someone tabling a motion but came out of discussions. It was agreed that there would be a two-year rolling programme to determine policy and that a national policy forum would be established. This would be made up of MPs and representatives from the regional committees, the unions and local government.

Tony wanted to get more people involved in the decision-making progress. The national policy forum produced documents, which were voted on every two years at the party conference. Policy commissions were set up to examine small areas of policy. I chaired a policy commission on transport. John Prescott, who was deputy prime minister, and in charge of transport, came along. He was always very knowledgeable. When someone joked that he would have to set an example on saving energy by driving a mini, he replied, 'There wouldn't be room for my wife's hair.'

The policy forum documents were sent to all the affiliated organizations, including the unions, and then discussed at that year's conference. This new system was harder work, as you had to read all the detail in the policy document. You couldn't just decide to do this or that. But initially the unions didn't twig that they should get involved in the drafting of the documents in order to influence the policy. This only happened a few years later. One thing the T&G succeeded in was persuading Labour not to abolish the agricultural wages boards.

The first national policy forum was held at the Ark building, overlooking Hammersmith flyover, and the second in Leeds. Others were held around the country, often at universities, because the accommodation was cheap and the meetings lasted two or three days.

Because the national policy commission was set up by the party, some MPs didn't bother engaging with it. Tony made it clear that he expected MPs and ministers to get involved to avoid the forum talking about one thing, while ministers talked about another thing.

The national policy forum was one of the best initiatives introduced by Labour, because, by and large, it was made up of people who knew what they were talking about. However, it was not universally liked by the unions, as they preferred the old way of putting resolutions to conference. It was less work and, as they saw it, brought instant results. The fact that much of the time nobody in the party followed up on the resolutions did not seem to come home to them. I think that the majority of NEC members who attended the national policy forum saw it, as I did, as a good place for developing policy, because it was made up of a broad spectrum of party activists. Yet, at the same time, the process was complicated, and one in which party members were often pulling in different directions. You had policy being made by 10 Downing Street and also by the national policy forum.

People often got confused about the differences between the government, the Labour Party and MPs. The Labour Party is an organization in itself. It provides all the support mechanisms. It was not the same as the government. The Labour Party is a political organization that supports the democratic process. It's the party that enables someone to become a member of parliament and it's the party that enables people at local level to hold that MP to account and to select and campaign for local councillors.

The NEC is the decision-making body of the Labour Party and consists of trade-union officials, representatives from the constituencies and socialist societies, and MPs. The four most senior positions on the NEC are the party leader, who was Tony Blair; the deputy leader (John Prescott); the general secretary (Tom Sawyer); and the treasurer (myself). The general secretary, not the party leader, is the most senior person on the NEC. The post is equivalent to that of a chief executive.

I found that the relationship between the chair of the party, the general secretary and the prime minister was tricky. In many ways, the general secretary is always in a hopeless position because he or she is answerable to the prime minister and to the NEC, and also trying to keep members happy and fundraisers on board.

You didn't need to be especially good with figures to be treasurer. I'm hopeless—Bill Morris had bought me an abacus after my appointment. But the post was more of a political figurehead. The director of finance, David Pitt-Watson, whom I used to meet regularly to go through the accounts, did the real number-crunching.

One of my jobs was to read out the treasurer's report at the annual party conference. This was always after the leader's speech, so the hall was nearly empty. To try and encourage members to stay to listen to it, David compiled a quiz with a bottle of champagne as a prize. You had to listen to the speech to get the answers. The hall remained quite full for a change. Someone from Hampstead and Highgate won the prize, which was a bit of an irony given that it's such a well-off area.

NEC meetings were held at the party HQ, which was then on Walworth Road. We all sat around a long table, which made it difficult to see the expressions on everyone's faces. Tony would stroll into the meeting and say, 'Hi, guys,' before taking his seat. He had a relaxed, cheerful approach. He would give an account of decisions that were being made and what was happening in parliament. Afterwards, everyone would ask questions and he would explain why certain things were being done. He didn't usually stay for the whole meeting. When he left, Gordon Brown, Mo Mowlam and most of the MPs would also go. I thought this was a very poor show. Margaret Beckett and Hilary Armstrong, on the other hand, always stayed for the entire meeting.

Tony wanted the unions to get the views of their members rather than present the views of the committee. But what he didn't recognize were the financial implications of this. I remember him saying at a One Member One Vote meeting that we should send a letter to all union members to get their views on a particular issue.

'Have you any idea what this would cost just to do one mailing?' asked Robin Cook, who was a member of One Member One Vote.

'What do you mean?' asked Tony.

'It would cost over a million pounds.'

Tony also didn't like what he saw as unnecessary bureaucracy. In 2001 myself, Maggie Jones, Margaret Wall, Margaret McDonagh and Charles Clarke had a meeting with him at Number Ten to discuss the salaries of five or six Downing Street staff who were paid by the party. Tony wanted to increase their pay. It was a sunny day, so he suggested we sit in the rose garden.

'We can't just increase their salaries,' I said. As I saw it to do this would go against the principles of negotiated pay agreements.

'Why?' asked Tony, looking irritated.

'Because they are employed by the party and they are on its pay scale. If we pay the staff at Downing Street more, what are the others on the same pay scale going to say? And anyway we don't have the money.'

'Well, in that case, I'll go out and raise the money myself,' he said.

We all thought this quite comical and wondered if he planned to go busking with his guitar.

The question it raised in Tony's mind was, who is in charge here? If he was leader of the party why couldn't he just decide what to do? Margaret McDonagh's problem, and mine, was that we had to report to conference that we had done everything to balance the books. Tony had no patience with what he saw as bureaucracy. If he decided to do something, he was determined to do it, no matter what others might say.

'Tell you what,' suggested Charles, 'you give us an amount of money to cover the party employees at Number Ten and we'll sort it out as we see fit.'

'OK, that seems to be the way round it,' I said. Charles' solution kept everyone happy. Tony got to increase the pay of the employees, but without it affecting the party's pay scale.

I remember that meeting for another reason. A few days before, I had arrived back from a trip to an ICEM conference near Rio de Janeiro in Brazil and my legs were covered in spots after being bitten to pieces by mosquitoes.

I'd gone there with Carol Bruce, the ICEM women's officer, to mark the end of a three-year training programme for women working in the pharmaceutical, chemical and rubber industries in South America. The women were taught things such as how to negotiate, deal with grievances, understand pay systems and develop self-confidence. It had been funded by the Scandinavian unions, which always seemed quite well off.

Carol and I were taken by a union representative and his wife to visit a union school outside Rio. But he got lost and we ended up driving through a *favela* on the hillside. All I could see around me were shacks with groups of very dodgy-looking youths staring at us as we drove past. I felt a little anxious, but then reassured myself that the union representative must know what he was doing.

But his wife didn't think so. 'We could all be killed!' she suddenly screamed.

'I know this area and these people,' he said.

'But we're in an expensive car!' she said.

We got out of the *favela* without incident, and a few days later, the couple took Carol and me for a wonderful lunch at a restaurant overlooking the sea in Copacabana in the south of the city. Our plates were piled so high with lobster, prawns and all sorts of fish that none of us could finish it. Just before we left, his wife called a waiter over and asked him for some boxes. I watched her scoop up the food into them, wondering what she was up to. When we got outside the restaurant, she gave a loud whistle and from nowhere all these street children appeared. They grabbed the boxes from her and disappeared again. It was extraordinary.

Tony and other senior figures in the Labour Party didn't trust Ken Livingstone. They saw the former GLC leader and MP for Brent East as an opportunist and someone who spelt trouble. His leftist politics didn't fit in with New Labour. So when he decided to stand as Labour candidate for Mayor of London to run the new Greater London Authority, there was consternation in the cabinet.

When the NEC met in October 1999 I suggested that we form an electoral college to select our candidate for Mayor of London. This was, I believed, the best way to keep Ken Livingstone out. The T&G agreed I should propose this idea. Using an electoral college, the vote would be shared between the MPs, unions and Labour Party members. If only party members voted, there was a good chance that Livingstone might be selected because of his popularity. He was very good at presenting himself as a man of the people. When Frank Dobson was selected as Labour candidate, Livingstone left the party and decided to run as an independent. And, as we all know, he won. I think if everyone had taken the GLA mayoral election more seriously from a much earlier stage, then we might have found a more plausible candidate. Ken had been campaigning quietly for years.

I had been used to the discipline of the TUC general council meetings, where the members would say what they had to say and that was it. And everyone didn't feel they had to speak on every issue. But on the NEC it seemed like everyone always had something to say about everything. The chair didn't control the meeting. There was sometimes dissent, often from those who formed the grassroots alliance, NEC members who represented the constituencies or who were part of a left-wing grouping, and the Trots. I called one member Feminist Against Laughter. She had absolutely no sense of humour.

At one meeting, I noticed that Matthew Taylor, the assistant general secretary, was reading a book. I couldn't believe it.

John Monks would never have allowed this at meetings of the TUC general council.

When we broke for a cup of tea, I said to him, 'If you're still reading that book when I give my treasurer's report, I shall remark on it, Matthew.'

'What do you mean?' he said.

'I can't believe you could be so rude.'

When we went back in the room to continue the meeting, he slipped the book back in his briefcase.

When you get to sit on illustrious bodies you eventually discover that, in fact, almost everyone is quite ordinary and has the same concerns as we all do. On the NEC there were some very clever people, but they all had flaws like everyone else. Some could talk the talk but had no idea how the real world operated.

Like all political parties, Labour has always had problems raising money. The decline in trade-union membership led to a fall in income. Some funding came from private donors, not all of them true Labour supporters. Some just wanted to be part of the action. Other income came from the annual conference, where we were able to attract some major exhibitors who paid a lot for a stand.

Politicians are very good at spending money, and the party had a habit of spending what it didn't have on the basis that someone would bail it out or the bank would extend the overdraft. This culture only changed when Ray Collins became general secretary and decreed that subscriptions and sales would pay running costs and money from donors, big or small, would pay for development.

When Labour took office it introduced a rule that individual donations to political parties of over £5,000 and corporate donations of over £50,000 had to be declared to the Electoral Commission. This was to make funding transparent. It was an admirable idea, but it had unintended consequences.

Many people who made a donation wanted it to remain confidential.

In November 1997 the party found itself facing accusations that it had accepted £1 million from Bernie Ecclestone, the president of the Formula One Group, to go soft on banning tobacco advertising in the sport. Ecclestone had previously given money to the Tories. The storm that broke over this was so unnecessary and ridiculous. It seemed obvious to me when the party took money from him that people were going to put two and two together and think this was why Labour went soft on tobacco advertising. Ecclestone wasn't a Labour supporter. I felt he was only giving the money to protect his own interests.

I said to Tony that we needed a way of spotting the political hot potatoes. He agreed and set up a funding committee. It was chaired by Ian McCartney, chairman of the party, and included David Triesman, the general secretary, Margaret Jay, Matthew Evans, Michael Levy and myself. If there were any concerns about a donor, the money was placed in a special holding account while enquiries were carried out into his or her background to see if there were any skeletons in the cupboard. If there was a question mark over the donor, then the money would be handed back.

But the committee never really did a very effective job. In part, this was because Michael Levy, who knew lots of wealthy people and was known as someone who could tap the shoulder, and had raised lots of money in the Jewish community for different causes, kept a lot of information to himself.

If someone made a donation over a certain amount, then the Electoral Commission published his or her name. But if they made a loan it wasn't made public. However, the House of Lords appointments committee raised questions about why some of these people who had made big donations and then turned them into loans were being put forward for peerages. A police investigation followed, but no evidence was found that anything unlawful had taken place.

I'm not against high-profile people donating money to political parties. It's true that some people only make large donations because they are expecting something in return. But on the other hand it doesn't seem right to exclude genuine supporters from a knighthood, peerage or other honours, because they have donated money to the party.

I was dragged into another controversy over donors in 2007, six years after I'd completed my term as treasurer, when it was revealed that the party had accepted £600,000 from the businessman David Abrahams. But the payments hadn't been made in Abrahams' name: they had been made via third parties, including a small builder and a secretary, which was against the rules governing party donations.

I was interviewed on BBC 2's *Newsnight* and made it clear in the interview with Martha Kearney that I was very annoyed with Jack Dromey for giving the impression it was everyone else's fault. He was the treasurer at the time and he should have discussed the donation with Peter Watt, the finance director. There was a view held by some that Jack went to the media in cahoots with Gordon Brown as they saw this as a way of damaging Tony Blair. At the very least it was known that Jack had met with Gordon Brown, Charlie Falconer and Ian McCartney, and between them they had agreed a plan of action. But Jack didn't stick to it. He had gone on Newsnight to say what a disgrace it all was and that he didn't know anything about it. This wasn't true. I don't know what Tony knew about this, but I'd be surprised if he knew anything.

Out of the blue in 2008 I was contacted by the police and asked to attend an interview. It took place in an anonymous office block in Buckingham Gate. I remember going through several sets of steel doors and thinking this was like something in a film. I was interviewed in a small room with two officers, one male and one female, who placed a spreadsheet listing party donations on the table. They wanted to know about some of the donors on the sheet and how the funding committee worked. I explained that, before any donations were accepted, Labour Party staff should have carried out background checks to ensure that there was nothing dodgy about the money. I pointed out that it was the job of the party staff, not the funding committee, to find out whether donations were from appropriate people.

I'd never been interviewed by the police before and, even though both officers were very polite, I found it a bit scary. When I left the interview I felt angry at being dragged into this. Not long afterwards, Margaret Jay, who had also been interviewed by the police, and I attended a meeting at Downing Street with John Mendelson, Gordon Brown's fundraiser, Roy Kennedy, the finance director, and several staff.

'This is not on,' I said. 'It's outrageous that Margaret and I should be interviewed by the police.'

I was amazed that none of them seemed to understand why we were so angry. They just sat there, looking baffled. When we came out Margaret and I were laughing because we had told them off. Neither of us cared very much what they thought of us. It was what we thought of ourselves and our reputations that really mattered.

It was clear that the party systems had not worked properly, either by default or by design. It took ages before the police told us the case had been dropped.

I don't think the Labour Party was very well run. It spent money it didn't have. When Bill Morris became general secretary of the T&G we embarked on a big cost-cutting exercise. We made staff redundant, closed some of our regional centres and sold off properties. But the Labour Party was always asking for more money.

When I saw an advertisement inviting applications to become a member of the central arbitration committee, which Labour had revamped to resolve disputes between management and workers over union recognition, I decided to apply. I was successful and joined it in April 2000. The committee, which met every few weeks at an office in Old Street, was chaired by Sir Michael Burton, a High Court judge, and was made up of academics and solicitors specializing in industrial law and representatives from business and the unions.

Unions affiliated to the party often sponsored an MP. Possible candidates were interviewed at regional and national level. If you became a T&G-sponsored MP you were likely to gain more votes. If someone could say they were sponsored by the T&G, then all the members in the constituency would be likely to vote for them. To get a foot in the door, it helped if an influential T&G official mentioned your name.

I don't know if I was that influential as national women's secretary, but I certainly received quite a few invitations to glitzy events at places such as Admiralty House and the US ambassador's residence in Regent's Park. In July 1999 Tony invited me for dinner at Chequers. I drove down on a Saturday afternoon and booked into a hotel in Aylesbury recommended by John Monks and then caught a taxi. Chequers is a lovely old house set in beautiful grounds. The other guests included David Frost, John Cleese and his wife, Rebekah Wade (who soon afterwards became editor of the *News of the World* and was later embroiled in the News International phone-hacking scandal) and her partner, the *East Enders* actor Ross Kemp, and Alan Milburn and his wife. Before dinner, we had a drink on the terrace, where we all made small talk. The catering service was provided by the Wrens.

After dinner, Cherie Blair took us on a tour of the house. A man who was involved with the Old Vic theatre was unimpressed by the décor chosen by Margaret Thatcher. He said, 'Oh, look at all this Laura Ashley. The V and A would have come up with something far better.'

I liked Cherie. I always found her straightforward and friendly, and she was lovely when she met our members. She was committed to fairness and human rights. Being the wife of a prime minister is not easy, as she revealed in her book *The Goldfish Bowl*. You are under scrutiny all the time and the media are always watching everything you do. In March 2001, she invited members of the TUC women's committee and senior women trade unionists to Number Ten for tea. We were standing there chatting in one of the rooms when she laughed and said, 'Here we are, all supposed to be movers and shakers, and we're talking about the nuisance of doing the washing by hand.'

However, someone I've never really got on well with is Clare Short. I remember her once kicking up such a fuss at one Labour Party conference just because Peter Mandelson took her seat in the seating reserved for MPs. She knew the TV cameras would catch her here. She complained to an NEC member and he offered her his seat on the platform. And she had the cheek to take it.

Despite the serious political issues that came up, there were many light moments during my time on the NEC. Ian McCartney was a very amusing speaker. I remember on one occasion he was regaling us with a story when I noticed John Prescott looking very grim. I whispered this to Mo Mowlam. She said, 'Well, he's got the hump because if this doesn't finish soon it's not going to make the one o'clock news.' Being an old hand at politics, John understood that you have to get your face on TV to stay in the mind of your constituents. There's no time for joking.

Charles Clarke was someone else who could be very amusing. He used to refer to Ian Duncan Smith, who was known as IDS when he was Tory leader, as 'In Deep Shit'. Charles also had a habit of turning up in a restaurant to join me and the three other Margarets—Margaret Wall, Maggie Jones and Margaret McDonagh—for a meal and leaving just before the bill arrived. I don't think he was mean. I just think it never occurred to him.

Like every new government, Labour changed the names of some of the departments. When the Department of Education became the Department of Children, Schools and Families, the staff used to refer to it as the Department for Cushions and Soft Furnishings.

I ended my stint on the NEC at the party conference in 2001. After the meeting on the Wednesday, when the new members of the NEC were introduced, Tony presented me with a certificate to mark the five years I had served.

'Thank you for all you've done,' he said, adding quietly, as he handed me the certificate, 'We'll have to find a way to thank you properly.'

I didn't know what he meant at the time, but I found out three years later.

12. Life at the Top

WHEN JACK ADAMS was coming up to retirement as T&G deputy general secretary in 1998, I decided that I would stand for the post. I felt that, having worked for the T&G for fifteen years, and being a national organizer, I was more than capable of being Bill's number two. And I knew that he wanted me to get the job, which was why he had supported my idea of organizing manufacturing conferences. Bill and Jack hadn't got on that well. Jack was an excellent negotiator. He had sorted out the British Airways dispute with the cabin crew and also a dispute involving the Liverpool dockers. But he wasn't good at strategy, or at knowing how to keep the union on side with the Labour Party.

Fred Higgs, who was head of the chemical workers and also worked at central office, announced that he was going to stand. Although he was an experienced official and a good negotiator, he was only known among the chemical workers, whereas union members in lots of different industries knew me. So while the textile workers and vehicle builders would have known me, they wouldn't have had a clue who Fred was. The only other candidates were Jim Bowie, an official from the north-west, and Khadem Hussein, a lay member who was virtually unknown.

The first thing I had to do was draw up a campaign. I wasn't allowed to use union funds or facilities to do this, so I formed a small group of supporters, which included Ray, Andrew Murray, the communications officer, and Jenny Smith, a political adviser to Bill. They agreed to help me because they believed in my ideas about the direction the union should take. In other words, they wanted to see a modern and forward-looking union. We planned our strategy sitting around the table in a pub round the corner from the T&G office.

The way the vote worked was that branches were asked to nominate a candidate. When central office sent out the ballot papers, it listed the branch numbers and the candidate they had nominated. This meant the members could see who the branches had chosen to support. For example, Ford in Dagenham had three or four branches. Two were right-wing and one was run by the Trots and was barking mad. So if you were nominated by the barking mad branch, members might think, 'Mm, I'm not sure about this candidate.'

If I was going to win the election, then it was vital that I got the broad left behind my campaign, as this would give it legitimacy with shop stewards and branches. And paid officers who agreed with the broad left would be expected to promote my campaign with the members by arranging meetings for me to speak at. The broad left was originally a political coalition between Labour and Communist Party members who fought to increase the power of the workers in the trade-union movement. Those on the broad left saw themselves as progressive and wanted nothing to do with the Trots, whom they saw as chancers and opportunists. They were sometimes known as 'entryists' because they infiltrated organizations and then tried to take over. The Socialist Workers' Party, which had managed to win over some white-collar workers, fell into this group. The collapse of the British Communist Party was a blow to trade unions within the big workplaces as they were very disciplined and, mostly, quite sensible.

I held a meeting in a community centre outside Manchester. I paid for the hire of it through contributions from those attending, a mixture of lay and paid members from across the country. John Aitken, who represented the engineers on the executive and was seen as a leader of the broad left, chaired it. It went well and I left feeling that I had done enough for John to support me publicly.

I launched my campaign on Wednesday 16 September in White's Bar in Blackpool, during the week of the TUC conference. I also held an afternoon tea at the hotel where I was staying, and around twenty union members turned up. Some years before, Diana Holland, the T&G national women's organizer, had started an afternoon women's tea to introduce women delegates to the way the conference worked. For someone going to a conference for the first time, it can be very confusing and complicated. The afternoon tea enabled women to get to know each other and understand how the voting and resolutions at the conference worked.

My daughter Stella and my granddaughter Hannah came to the conference with me. Hannah wandered around giving out leaflets with 'Look to the Future with Margaret' written on them, and putting yellow and black 'Vote Margaret Prosser' stickers on delegates.

I went on the campaign trail, visiting workplaces up and down the country. I tried to combine this with my official visits as national organizer. It was even more hectic than when I was TUC president. Often shop stewards who were going to support me invited me to a branch dinner. When I look at my diary from that period, I'm amazed at how I managed to fit so much in. I could not have done this without my secretary, Louisa Manning. When I was out of the office for days at a time, she ran the show at central office, dealing with my correspondence and making sure any requests were answered promptly and efficiently. Louisa was a single parent who had arrived in London from the West Indies when she was young. When she first started with me, I agreed that she could leave the office each day at 3.30 p.m. to collect her daughter from the primary school around the corner and bring her back to the office. She was an incredibly well-organized person and a rock for me.

I remember going to the south-west, a highly unionised area and regarded as quite radical. It was where the Tolpuddle Martyrs came from. Although much of it is rural, there's also a lot of industry there. I visited a factory where they made the nose cone for Concorde, another where they made electrical fittings for the insides of cabins on planes, British Cellophane in Taunton, and a company that made garage doors. When a production manager is showing you complicated electronic systems you have to look interested. But there is only so much you can say about a garage door. 'Oh, it comes in red, does it?' But I did my best, as the shop stewards were always proud to have a visit from a national official.

I also spoke to a couple of thousand stewards at a festival in Taunton organized by the T&G. At Gate Gourmet, which produces trays of food for airlines, near Heathrow Airport, the senior official said in Punjabi to the mainly Asian workers that I was the person they should vote for. They all bowed their heads. At Sky Chefs, another company producing airline food, I spent a couple of hours with the workers on the picket, as the new owners, a US company, had locked them out.

When I visited a cooker factory in the north-west, some of the women greeted me by holding up their hands. On the white gloves they were wearing they had written 'Vote Margaret'.

The management at Golden Wonder in Sheffield gave me several boxes of crisps. I left them in the car overnight near the hotel I stayed in. When I got into the car the following morning to drive to a glass factory in Rotherham, the smell was awful.

Other visits I made included the Atomic Weapons Establishment near Reading; the Royal Ordnance factory in Bishopton, Scotland; Tunnock's teacake factory in Glasgow, where the owner liked to park his Rolls Royce outside the main entrance; a chicken factory somewhere in rural Ireland; and Waterford Glass.

On the May Bank Holiday I attended a truckfest—a road transport festival—in Peterborough. The trucks, which were all painted with fancy designs in bright colours, were parked in a large field. The event was like a country show with tents and stalls selling all kinds of stuff. The Scottish football international Ally McCoist did a demonstration of his skills. The T&G had a stall, as we were the main union for truck drivers. The crowds were so huge that it took ages to get out of the car park.

Nominations closed on 22 October. When I discovered that more branches had nominated me than the other candidates, I felt that my chances of winning must be very good. What surprised me was how many nominations I had received from region two, the south-west. All those visits I has made there had really paid off.

I felt exhausted when the campaign ended. My abiding memory of that period is standing on a windy platform at some railway station or other, my briefcase between my feet, staring expectantly down the track, hoping my train would arrive soon and wishing I had put on a warmer jacket.

Voting commenced on 9 November and the result was announced on 11 December at the offices of the Electoral Reform Society in north London. I drove up there with Bill and Ray. As soon as we walked in, I felt confident I'd won. Looking at the piles of ballot papers with my name on, which were stacked on long tables, I could see that mine were much higher than those of the four other candidates. When the results were read out, I had won by a large majority.

Margaret Prosser 50,721
Fred Higgs 39,344
Alan James Bowie 22,930
Khadem Hussein 7,445

This was the first time in the T&G's history that a woman had been elected deputy general secretary. I felt very proud. The following evening the T&G central office team organized a party at the Marquis of Granby pub in Smith Square, and we had a thoroughly good night.

Being a deputy is a funny job. When anyone asked what a deputy general secretary did, I always replied, 'Whatever the general secretary says.' If the general secretary doesn't like you, then you will find yourself in the canteen making sandwiches. I phoned Brendan Barber, deputy general secretary of the TUC, and told him that when Senator John McCain lost the Republican US presidential nomination to George W. Bush in 2000 someone asked him if he would run to be vice-president. 'Certainly not,' he said. 'The job of the vice-president is to tell the president several times a day how well he looks and to represent the president at the funerals of Third World leaders.'

'Is that accurate, Brendan?' I asked.

'It's spot on,' he said.

We had a good laugh.

As I've previously mentioned, I had a lot of respect for Bill and he had always encouraged me in what I was doing. If I had an idea, I would always send him a note rather then telling him face-to-face in his office, as this made it easier for him to think about it. At the same time, I always felt he never quite trusted me. He always seemed to hold back. Both Ray Collins and I said that we worked with him for twenty years but didn't feel any closer to him at the end than we did at the beginning. I think Bill has always found it hard to open up and be close to anybody.

When the T&G decided to leave Palace Street in Victoria and buy a building on Theobald's Road, the week before we were due to move in, Bill, Ray and I went to have a look at how the refurbishment was going. When we opened the door into Bill's new office on the sixth floor, Bill stood there, looking stunned. Compared to his office in Palace Street, it was tiny. He needed a large office because he often met there with senior officials or visitors. He was so angry he was unable to speak. He gave orders for the office to be enlarged and took over my office, which had been completed. This meant that Louisa and I had to work downstairs in one of the committee rooms until the building work was completed. I could understand Bill needing a larger office, but I wasn't very happy at being slung out of my nice room and shunted downstairs.

Bill was really into diet and exercise. He always had a bowl of fruit on his desk and would munch on an apple as soon as he arrived each morning. He also went running. When we went out to a restaurant he was always very careful what he ordered, but then at the end of the meal he would eat lots of cheese or all the chocolates on the small plate. He enjoyed hosting lunches at his house in Hemel Hempstead, where he lived with Eileen, who was a wonderful cook. Bill was a member of Cleo Lane's and Humphrey Littleton's jazz club in Hertfordshire, and he took Ray and me there a couple of times.

As deputy general secretary I was responsible for all the T&G members, including those in Gibraltar, and I made several trips there. There's not much in Gibraltar apart from the port and the tiny high street. Although it's so close to Spain, it feels very English. Most of the members worked in the docks, in the hospitals or on the council. Central office didn't have a clue about what they were doing. It was so far off the beaten track. For example, the office closed for much of the afternoon, which meant that if any members needed help they couldn't get it. I met with the governor of Gibraltar a couple of times to make sure that he would consult beforehand with the union if he was proposing any major changes on the island.

We also had members in the Channel Islands and on the Isle of Man. After a trip to Jersey, I said to Bill, 'The members on the islands aren't getting a fair deal from us.'

'What do you mean?'

'Well, a lot of the materials we produce nationally don't apply to them.' Although the islands are crown dependencies, they often have different laws on issues such as maternity leave.

'So what do you think we should do?'

I told him that we should form a council for the islands and produce separate materials for them. Our research department could find out the different laws they had.

Bill though this was a brilliant idea. So to make the members feel more involved, I organized meetings in the different islands. And they were a great success.

Following the fall of the Berlin Wall in 1989, many union officials began travelling to Eastern Europe. In 1991 I had visited Hungary and Czechoslovakia. What had struck me was that the women we had met in the factories didn't think the end of Communism would mean that the employment conditions would change. They didn't understand that under capitalism it was all about making money and that things such as a crèche, maternity leave and summer holidays might well disappear unless they organized themselves into an independent union.

I had been shocked at how grim some of the factories were. In one place in Budapest that processed catgut to make tennis rackets, the women worked with hardly any lighting. Some of them felt very bitter about having to work full-time when they also had to run a home and look after children. One said, 'At weekends we have to bottle fruit and vegetables from our gardens because we haven't got fridges.' Another explained how hard it was to find shoes in the shops. I came away from my trips to Eastern Europe thinking that many people on the left in Britain had glorified Communism. The reality of it was that women had to struggle to live in exactly the same way my mum had done after the Second World War.

These memories were still fresh in my mind when I flew to Moscow with Carol Bruce, the women's officer for ICEM, in April 1999. Although everyone in Russia was a union member, the unions were really run by the management, not the workers. They weren't independent, as they are in the UK. The purpose of our visit was to explain what a union could provide for its members and encourage them to get involved in union activities.

We were met at the airport by a woman on the ICEM executive, who was waiting in a huge limousine to take us to a union school, where we would be staying. When I stepped out of the airport the temperature dropped immediately. It was absolutely freezing. The school was a run-down place and the staff who worked there were very surly and unhelpful. The food was awful. One morning we had cold liver and cold rice for breakfast. The bread that was served at breakfast was left in a basket on the table until the evening meal, by which time it was as hard as rock.

We were introduced to a group of workers in the chemical and pharmaceutical industries. Carol told me that these were the people who had previously made chemical weapons. They now worked in factories that made things such as plastics and dyes. They were very educated. Before the meeting began all the delegates said who their favourite poets and composers were. I thought to myself, if you asked this at a T&G meeting, no one would know what to say. We spoke about the importance of health and safety, and of making sure workers received paid holidays and had legal help.

Our interpreter, Valentina, a lovely woman who spoke perfect English, took us to see Red Square and the Kremlin. I had always thought the Kremlin was one building but, in fact, it's a complex of buildings. When we joined a long queue at a kiosk to change some money, a soldier whispered to Valentina that he would change it for us. She shook her head and looked very anxious. She wasn't prepared to break the rules.

Yet Moscow seemed a grey, miserable city. I didn't like it and I didn't feel comfortable.

'You know what,' I said to Carol as we sat in the departure lounge waiting for our flight home, 'I can't wait to get on our plane.'

'Why?'

'So that I can see someone smile.'

In October of that year, I flew to Durban in South Africa for the ICEM conference, which was held in a different city every four years. I was part of a ten-strong UK delegation. The trip was a total contrast to our visit to Moscow. The weather was warm and sunny and everyone in the streets seemed cheerful. We stayed in a fantastic hotel on the seashore. The Hindu feast of Diwali was being celebrated. In the evening, the road the hotel stood on was decorated with lights, and crowds wandered along it, buying food and sweets from dozens of stalls. Despite the ending of apartheid, you could see that the top jobs were still occupied by whites. The Indians had the next best jobs and the blacks were at the bottom of the pile.

One day we went on a solidarity march through the centre of the city. Unlike the march I'd been on in Santiago, this one was peaceful and celebratory. Everyone was wearing T-shirts and carrying union banners.

At an ICEM meeting at Cairns in Australia in 1997 I had suggested that every region should have a seat for a woman, but my motion had been rejected. I was more hopeful of getting it accepted in Durban. The chairman, a German, was on our side and he argued our case very persuasively with various delegations.

On the morning at the conference that was devoted to discussing the rules of ICEM, Thabo Mbeki, the president of South Africa, arrived. He had worked for a trade union organization and everyone thought he would be progressive. But he turned out to be a disappointment, especially with his views on HIV.

There must have been about forty delegates from Japan, all men apart from the interpreters. During the afternoon session at the conference they all fell asleep.

I was delighted when the conference voted to accept my motion. I felt this was another small but important victory for women in the trade-union movement. Carol then came into the hall with her arms full of roses and began handing them out to delegates. As she walked around giving them out, everyone clapped and cheered and all the South African women burst into song.

I arrived back in London to discover that *Good Housekeeping* magazine had named me among the hundred most influential women in the UK. I was listed tenth; I felt very flattered.

Women were certainly becoming more influential in society. In 2001 The Guardian had carried an article with the headline 'The Four Margarets', pointing out that the four most important positions in the Labour Party were all held by women called Margaret. I was treasurer, Margaret McDonagh was general secretary, Maggie Jones was chair and Margaret Wall was vice-chair.

But there was still discrimination going on, as the case of Fiona Marshall in 1998 illustrated. Fiona Marshall, the women's officer in Northern Ireland, took the T&G to a tribunal after applying for a more senior post and failing to get it. She suspected this was because it had been decided before the interview to give the job to someone else. The deputy general secretary at the time, two members of the executive, and the regional secretary decided on appointments. And the person the regional secretary wanted always got the job. No one had received any equality or discrimination training.

A lot of members tried to persuade Fiona to drop the case, as it wasn't the done thing to go public on an issue like this. But I was very public in my support of her. Bill also supported her. Neither of us liked the idea of the union being embarrassed, but we felt this was the only way to end this practice and make the system fair.

One senior union official said to me, 'You don't use the law, Margaret. You fight your battles inside.'

'Well, we've been trying to fight this battle inside for years and it hasn't worked,' I said.

When I met Fiona at a hotel during a trip to Belfast, I told her to carry on with her case, no matter what other union officials said to her. She did. And she won. The tribunal castigated the union for its shoddy arrangements and for not being transparent. This didn't surprise me one bit, as it had a terrible record in making sure appointments were decided fairly.

Afterwards, Bill and I insisted in an executive council meeting that anyone involved in making appointments had to be trained. We brought in a company called Equality Works, recommended by Ray Collins. It trained all of our executive council members, national officers, regional secretaries and anyone else involved in recruitment, showing them things such as how to write person specifications and job descriptions, and how to interview candidates. From there on, only those who had been on the course could take part in the recruitment process. But some of the regional secretaries couldn't see why they needed training.

One of them said to me, 'Well, you benefited from job fixing when you got the national organizer job.'

He was right. I did. And I knew it, and wasn't proud of it.

But something I am proud of during my four years as deputy general secretary is giving women a greater voice on the industrial committees. When I had been national organizer I gave the industrial groups targets for including more women on their committees. This started the ball rolling, but it didn't really work, as I couldn't force the union officials to include more women.

Diana Holland, the national women's organizer, and I drew up a proposal for proportionality on the industrial committees. We said that industrial groups must include a number of women on their local and national committees proportional to the number of women members. The food and drink committee and the passenger committee, for example, would have to have a higher percentage of women members than the dockers' committee. As well as this change, every region was given an extra seat on the executive council, and this seat had to be given to a woman.

By now I had a high profile both in the union and in the Labour Party. In 1999 I was invited to serve on the Equal Pay Task Force, which was set up by the Equal Opportunities Commission. The human resources director of BT, which paid for the secretariat, chaired it and we met at BT's offices in the City. I didn't feel the task force was going to achieve anything, as it didn't have any political backing. It operated in isolation. We produced a report, *Just Pay*, criticizing the lack of commitment by employers, unions and government to closing the pay gap and called for a law to force employers to carry out regular equal pay reviews, a transparent pay process to root out inequality, and an end to the job segregation that leads to women ending up in undervalued and underpaid jobs. But the report never went anywhere.

I was also appointed as a non-executive member of the Fair Markets Board, part of the DTI. The board met in the basement of the DTI offices in Victoria Street and discussed issues such as employment law, health and safety, and Europe. The idea was that people from outside the civil service would give their thoughts and bring their experience. There were three other members, including a woman who ran a business in the north and a woman who went on to become chief executive of the Joseph Rowntree Foundation. We discussed issues such as supporting small businesses and the performance assessment of staff. The civil service, of course, are very good at monitoring and measuring. The department used scorecards to track the effectiveness of policies. These were operated on what was known as the RAG system (red, amber, green).

The RAG system is designed to alert board members and/or the responsible member of staff to the progress, or non-progress, of a piece of work. All work areas are costed and timed and reports are given at regular intervals to the board. Red means the work is behind schedule, amber means it needs careful watching, green means it is on track.

I think advisory boards like this are a good idea, but there are senior civil servants who are against them. One civil servant, who was responsible for health and safety, couldn't see the point of bringing in people such as me. But the director of the Fair Markets Division was very enthusiastic and saw the value of what we did. Unfortunately, his career in the civil service ended when a national newspaper alleged that he had taken his girlfriend on an official trip to China at the taxpayer's expense.

In 2000 the TUC nominated me to sit on the Low Pay Commission, an independent public body set up under the National Minimum Wage Act 1998 to advise the government about the minimum wage. Because this was a statutory body, it would have real impact. The chair when I joined was Sir George Bain, then vice-chancellor of Queen's University in Belfast and a former director of the London Business School. Other members included the dean of one of the Cambridge colleges and an academic from the LSE. It was a number-crunching committee. We received evidence about pay from the Low Pay Unit, the Office of National Statistics, employers' organizations, think tanks and civil servants. We met either at the DTI or at an office in the West End. Once a year, when we were producing the annual report, we travelled to a country house in Oxford for an away day.

Adair Turner, a big noise at Merrill Lynch, succeeded Sir George. He is the cleverest person I have ever met. He would come into a meeting and look through pages of figures and understand them immediately.

Mind you, he wasn't streetwise. We had a discussion about farm labourers and the minimum wage. We had evidence that some labourers were being charged nearly all their wages by their employers for living in some grotty room. We were talking about what to do about gangmasters when Adair looked across at me and said, 'What is a gangmaster?' The committee thought this was quite funny. But if Adair didn't understand something, he always made it his business to find out about it.

On another occasion, when someone from the Federation of Hairdressers was talking to us, Adair said, 'I'm not really following you.'

I said, 'He's talking about not paying the right amount of tax.'

He looked astonished when I said this.

For example, one of the problems hairdressers had was that when they took on youngsters they had to pay them the national minimum wage, even though they weren't bringing in any money.

Security guards were a group that had always been very poorly paid and subject to some very bad practices. When I met some of them at a shopping centre in Belfast, they told me that the minimum wage had helped hugely because it had improved standards in the industry.

It's always nice to have your hard work acknowledged. In 2002 I received the Barbara Castle Award from the government's Women's Equality Unit at a ceremony at Number Ten. It was given to me for my lifetime contribution to equality and equal pay. I was extremely touched.

Of course, I had to fit in the Low Pay Commission with my work at the T&G. It was agreed that I would represent the union at the Labour Party national policy forum, which was meeting at Durham University on the same weekend that the T&G's biannual policy conference was convening in Bournemouth. The plan was for me to go alone to Durham on the Friday and then on the Sunday fly from Newcastle to London, where a T&G official would meet me and drive me down to Bournemouth.

Bill had made a secret agreement with Gordon Brown that the T&G would withdraw its motions on the reconnection of the state retirement pension to wages from the Labour Party national policy forum agenda. Gordon didn't want pensions increased, as this would put more pressure on his economic policies. The T&G had campaigned for many years to bring back the link between wages and the state pension. Jack Jones had been in the forefront of this. My job was to go to Durham to persuade the other unions to agree to back Bill's decision. I knew this would be very tricky.

On the Thursday before I travelled to Durham I was due to attend a meeting of the joint policy committee at Number Ten. The committee, which was made up of cabinet and senior union figures, had to decide what to discuss at the National Policy Forum. The meeting would provide me with an opportunity to begin quietly trying to persuade the unions to support Bill's move to abandon the proposal restoring the link between wages and pensions at that stage.

When I arrived at the office early on Thursday morning, I bumped into Bill in the corridor. He said he wanted me to attend the finance and general purposes committee meeting later in the day.

'I can't go to the finance and general purposes committee because I have to go to the joint policy committee,' I said.

'Come to my office,' he said, looking very serious.

I followed him, wondering what the problem was.

'You need to start putting the industrial agenda before the political agenda,' he said, closing the door.

'Look, Bill, you've given me this job to do in Durham. It's going to be very difficult. I need to be at the joint policy committee to start talks with the other unions. Otherwise how am I going to get anyone on side?'

I can't remember what he replied, but I do remember that he just rattled on about me not putting the union first. I think he didn't like the fact that I was able to move easily between my union work and my work on the NEC. I've always been good at steering a middle path in everything I've done.

In the end, my patience wore out and I said, 'You know what, you're like a schoolboy.'

Bill looked shocked and said, 'I think you'd better leave the room.'

I stormed out, wondering what on earth was the matter with him. When I told Ray what had happened, he went to see Bill and explained the importance of me going to the joint policy committee. He took over the finance and general purposes committee.

When I arrived at Number Ten, I was very anxious about how I was going to persuade people such as Margaret Wall, Maggie Jones and others to get support from their own unions to support Bill's agreement with Gordon Brown. Because of Jack Jones, the T&G had always been seen as the leading light in campaigning for pensions to be linked to wages. When I explained what Bill was intending, they were aghast.

'What's he doing that for?' asked Maggie.

'Don't ask me,' I said. 'He's agreed it with Gordon.' Bill got on better with Gordon than Tony. I think this was because Gordon took more notice of him than Tony and used him more.

That evening, I travelled to Cardiff to attend a farewell dinner for George Wright. Early the following morning, I caught the train to London and then a train up to Durham for the National Policy Forum. I did my best to persuade the other union leaders to back Bill. It was up to the T&G if we wanted to withdraw the proposal, which was in our name. What we needed was for the other unions not to raise an argument about it in the open meeting.

On Sunday when the policy forum was finished a T&G officer picked me up at the university and drove me to Newcastle Airport. By now, I was feeling shattered. When I handed my ticket to the woman at the check-in desk, she studied it closely and then said, 'This ticket is for yesterday.'

'Oh,' I said. I was completely astonished, but so tired that I couldn't think straight.

'The plane is full. But you can go on the reserve list for the next flight, but we already have people on the list.'

I decided it would be better to take the train. Luckily I had some cash on me, so I went outside and hailed a cab. I phoned the union official who was meant to be meeting me at Heathrow and told him to meet me instead at King's Cross station. It was gone midnight by the time I arrived at my hotel in Bournemouth. I was exhausted and just crashed out on the bed. When I met Bill the next morning he was as nice as pie. He knew he had been in the wrong.

Not discussing pensions and wages at the National Policy Forum backfired. A few months later at the Labour Party conference the issue came up. Margaret McDonagh, the party general secretary, and myself were asked to meet Gordon in his hotel room. He was sitting there with Ed Balls.

Gordon was annoyed that the pensions issue had surfaced. 'So what are we going to say about pensions?' he snapped.

'Well, you should have dealt with it at the National Policy Forum,' I said, thinking he shouldn't expect Margaret and me to get him out of the hole he had dug himself into. I then suggested we followed the TUC practice in situations like this and say we make no recommendation and let the conference make its own mind up.

'Are you saying you're not prepared to support the Chancellor?' said Ed Balls.

'Don't talk to me about not supporting Labour. I've been supporting Labour longer than you have,' I said, thinking he had a right bloody cheek to try and make out I wasn't a loyal member of the party.

In the end, we got Jack Jones to withdraw the issue from the agenda. I remember Ray chasing Jack around the conference trying to get him to sign this bit of paper. He knew that if he didn't get Jack's signature he would have denied it afterwards. If Jack hadn't agreed to withdraw it, no one else would have agreed. Gordon agreed to establish a commission to examine the question of wages and pensions, and Jack was appointed to it.

I never found Gordon as straight as Tony. He would come to T&G conferences and made a tub-thumping speech and everyone would cheer to the rafters. But afterwards we would realize that he never said anything concrete. It was the same when he made a speech at the T&G's seventy-fifth anniversary celebration, held at Brown's restaurant in St Martin's Lane. He sounded very good, but he never promised anything or committed himself to anything.

Not long after Labour had been re-elected in 2001, Bill called me into his office.

'Margaret, I'm going to ask you to make a big sacrifice?'

'What's that?'

'I want Jimmy Elsby to replace you on the Labour Party NEC to raise his profile.' Bill wanted Jimmy, an assistant general secretary and the former regional secretary in Scotland, to succeed me as deputy general secretary when I retired.

This was fine by me. I'd done five years on the NEC, so I was quite happy to give it up. It involved a lot of work. But

I didn't think Jimmy was the right person to be deputy general secretary or to sit on the NEC. Also, he wasn't really interested in the NEC. Bill's decision to give Jimmy my position on the NEC got him into hot water with some of the other unions, because he had broken the unwritten rules. I had been given a seat on the NEC not only because I was a T&G member but also because I was an active member of the Labour Party. The seat didn't belong to the T&G. It existed because of an agreement made by a number of the big unions.

When Bill and I went to the Scottish TUC conference in April we had a big discussion about Jimmy going on the NEC with John Edmonds, general secretary of the GMB, and Dave Prentis, general secretary of Unison.

At the TUC conference in Brighton that year a rumour went around late in the morning of 11 September that something terrible had happened in New York. By lunchtime we had all seen the awful TV pictures of planes flying into the World Trade Centre, but it was still not clear what had happened. We didn't learn the full horror until later that afternoon.

Tony Blair was due to speak at the conference, but because of the terrible events in New York he needed to be at Number Ten. He said a few brief words to delegates and then left. The conference was adjourned and that night's presidential dinner was cancelled. I felt quite sorry for Bill, who was the TUC president that year, as the dinner at the end of your year as president is a big thing. The next morning the conference was disbanded, as it would have felt wrong to be arguing about resolutions when the USA had been plunged into chaos.

I retired from the T&G on 22 August 2002, my birthday, after nineteen years. I was sixty-five. A couple of weeks later, a dinner was held for me at Renaissance Hotel in Holborn. It was a wonderful occasion, and very glamorous. There was a harpist, a quartet and a DJ. The comedian Hattie Hayridge was the MC. The guests included my family and friends, some of the Red Ramblers, and close colleagues from the T&G and the Labour Party. Tony and Cherie Blair also turned up. In his speech, Tony said, 'Margaret has often given me advice in the past and foolishly on some occasions I didn't take it, and should have done.' Too right, I thought, smiling to myself.

The T&G produced a booklet with messages from many people including John Monks, Margaret Beckett, Patricia Hewitt and the *Woman's Hour* presenter Jenny Murray. Bill and I had had our ups and downs, but he was very generous in his message. He wrote, 'If anyone could deal with some of the extremes of the male-dominated trade-union world then Margaret was that woman.' Despite our not always seeing eye-to-eye, he had always been very supportive.

Because I had to take my sister Marion, who was in a wheelchair, back to her hotel, I didn't stay too late. The T&G had generously put up her, my sister Pam, my son and daughters and their partners and children in a hotel. When we left, the party was still in full swing. I left in pretty good order—I didn't have a drink until after I had made my speech—but I'm sure there were a few sore heads the morning after.

13. Bridging the Gap

IT'S AN ODD FEELING when you retire. After working for so many years at the T&G, I felt as if I had come out of long-term care. Who was going to provide me with my daily newspaper? Who was going to fill the car up with petrol? Who was going to write my letters? As a senior union figure, I had not had to do any of these things for many years. Sitting in the kitchen of my flat in Beckenham, I thought to myself, 'What will I say now when people ask me what I do?' I'm one of those people whose job is their life. Some people might want to put their feet up when they retire, but I didn't. After my three children had grown up, I always defined myself through my work. It's not just men who do this, as is commonly thought. Plenty of women do as well.

My weeks wouldn't be completely empty. I was still on the central arbitration committee and the employment appeal tribunal, but these wouldn't take up that much time. I'd now officially finished serving on the ICEM committee, although, a few weeks after retiring, I attended the ICEM women's conference in Bucharest, where the official who opened the conference turned to us and said, 'How lovely it is to see a sea of such pretty faces,' which, unsurprisingly, produced lots of raised eyebrows among the women delegates. So what would I do? What kind of opportunities was I going to find at sixty-five? If I'm honest, I felt quite empty inside.

A few months later, I was still feeling at a loose end, although I was visiting my children and friends more, when I was told about a vacancy for chair of the Women's National Commission. The Women's National Commission had been established in the 1960s under the government of Harold Wilson and was the official body that brought the voices of women in the UK to government and the voice of government to women. It also had an important role in bringing the views of non-governmental organizations to the UN Commission on the Status of Women conference, which I'd attended when it met in Beijing in 1995. I decided to apply for the post, as it was right up my street. A few weeks later, I was appointed.

The commission was an umbrella body for around 300 organizations in Britain. It was staffed by civil servants and responsible to the Secretary of State for Women, at that time Patricia Hewitt. There were no big names on the committee, just what you might call hard-working backroom women from organizations such as the National Federation of Women's Institutes, the Union of Catholic Mothers and the League of Jewish Women. When we met, we discussed issues such as pension rights, employment and achieving better access for women in public life. We provided the government with vital information on many issues, both in the UK and overseas. For instance, we established a Muslim women's group, which helped the government forge links with the Muslim community, and we ran a programme for women from Iraq to learn about democracy.

The commission provided me with a focus for my energy and enthusiasm, and it also enabled me to attend the UN Commission on the Status of Women conference at the UN headquarters in New York in 2004.

Sadly, the Women's National Commission was disbanded in 2011, when it had 450 organizations affiliated to it, as part of the Tory government's so-called 'bonfire of the quangos'. I for one will never forgive David Cameron for this act of government vandalism. It was listed as saving the government £1 million a year, but some other body will have to be paid to do the statutory work it carried out for the UN and other organizations.

Despite enjoying my time on the commission, I still missed union work. One morning in April 2004, Tom Sawyer, whom I knew from when he worked at NUPE and from when he had been general secretary of the Labour Party, phoned.

He told me he had conducted an inquiry into industrial relations at Royal Mail and one of his recommendations was that partnership committees should be set up between the union and the employer to improve industrial relations. For years, industrial relations at Royal Mail had been pretty bad and they had worsened when a modernization programme began.

'How would you fancy chairing an area partnership committee in East London?' he said.

'I'd love to, Tom.' I didn't need to think about it. This would get me back into the cut and thrust of negotiating that I loved so much.

The meetings were held at the mail centre in Bromley-by-Bow. Everything seemed to be going well at first, but then the Communication Workers' Union fell out with the Royal Mail over some proposal to change the national agreement.

In 2004 I was given the kind of challenge I had been hoping for when Tony Blair asked me to chair a commission examining the causes of the continuing gender pay and opportunities gap This was the first enquiry of the kind since the Equal Pay Act came into force in 1975. Sally Morgan, a political adviser to Tony, and Nita Clark, Tony's trade-union link, put my name forward. Number Ten had a dilemma. There was a National Policy Forum meeting coming up and one of the ideas being put forward was that every employer would have to conduct an equal pay audit. The Labour cabinet were against this, though, so in order to bat it away they agreed with the trade unions to launch an enquiry into the continuing causes of the gender pay gap.

I met with Sally and Nita at Number Ten to decide on who should sit on the commission and we agreed that it should include representatives from the TUC, the CBI, local government, small businesses, the Equal Opportunities Commission, the NHS, education and adult training.

We were originally asked to sit for one year but it took eighteen months to complete the work. We decided not to conduct any new research but instead to invite those who had already done research to present their findings to us. We invited academics and organizations working with women to make presentations. The civil servants who provided support were brilliant, making sure everything got written up, and an economist was loaned to us to help us grapple with all the numbers.

I went out to see some of the organizations that were trying to improve the situation for women. I remember an amazing project on a Glasgow housing estate that provided both childcare and opportunities for women to learn new skills. I heard a number of inspiring stories of women who had retrained. For example, I met a young woman who had worked in a shoe shop after leaving school—because the career adviser had suggested this—and then got married and had three children. She was given training by the organization and now runs her own IT company.

Another excellent organization that came to see us was called Women Like Us, run by two women in north London, who have since then both received the OBE. They began talking about work to other women at the school gates and then did some research and met with employers. The DTI gave them a grant and now they run an agency finding employment for women. Computer Clubs for Girls, which developed computer programmes aimed at girls, was another wonderful project.

I've always believed that providing young people with this sort of training is vital for the economy in Britain and for creating a skilled workforce. University isn't for everyone. Many young people who don't go to university are just as smart as those who do. I never went to university. Lots of young people would benefit far more by going on an apprenticeship scheme and learning a trade.

The Women and Work Commission report, *Shaping a Fairer Future*, was published in February 2006 and launched at Number Ten by Tony. It contained forty recommendations aimed at government and employers. It stressed that there was no magic bullet for improving the gender pay gap. We acknowledged that policies such as equal pay reviews might well have a part to play, but the evidence showed that lack of educational chances and of good-quality part-time jobs were major obstacles. Another problem was employment downsizing, whereby women returning to work after having children found themselves having to take lower level jobs to fit in with their family responsibilities and pay a big chunk of their earnings for childcare. While some women might afford to pay the costs of childcare for one child, they often couldn't pay for two.

One of the recommendations of the report was for more training and up-skilling of women who had fallen into lower-level jobs in order to accommodate children's needs. The report estimated that the Chancellor lost between £16 and £23 million each year because of women's reduced spending power.

I was now a member of the House of Lords. More about this later. I invited Ed Balls to the Lords for coffee. He had just become an MP. I had forgiven him for suggesting that I wasn't a loyal Labour member. I'm sure he didn't even remember it.

I said, 'There are far too many women who have children and can't afford to stay in their regular jobs, so end up in Marks and Spencer or Sainsbury's, working well below their capacity, because the retail trade offers choice on hours and days. But the pay is low.'

'So what's the answer?' he asked.

'Well, I think we need to a programme to enable these women to gain new skills.'

He spoke to Gordon about it.

The following month, Gordon announced the budget and I received a phone call from one of the civil servants attached to the commission.

'Guess what?'

'What?'

'Gordon has allocated £40 million for the training programme.'

I was overjoyed. It turned out that Gordon had allocated the money to pay for women-only workplace training delivered via the Sector Skills Councils, which allocated money to employers. The programme was refunded over five years and more than 24,000 women went through it across various sectors of the labour market. Some of the food companies trained women to become food technologists, while another organization took unemployed women and trained them to be bus drivers. When I went to an award ceremony at a hotel in Coventry held by LANTRA, which provides training for those working in the agriculture sector. I met women who had trained to be beekeepers, use chain saws, carry out artificial insemination and make cider. What a mix!

When the coalition government was elected it scrapped women-only training. This was short-sighted. Three reports into the programme were produced by Leeds Metropolitan University that hailed it as a huge success both with employers and those who received training. I am very proud of what the programme achieved.

Many people think the equal pay problem is about women being paid less than men for doing the same job. In some sectors, in finance, for example, this can be the case. But mostly it's not about this. It's about the social structure not being there to enable women to take part in the world of work in a way that acknowledges their abilities and needs, with good-quality part-time jobs, flexible working hours and affordable childcare.

At the last minute, Gordon Brown asked to attend the launch of *Shaping a Fairer Future*. But we didn't know if we had enough space, as the room was small and our guest list was already full. However, we decided we couldn't have him standing outside the door, so we squeezed him in. Tony spoke about the report in glowing terms, stressing that Labour was committed to improving the pay and conditions for working women.

During the time we put the report together I had been in and out of Number Ten all the time to make sure we were on the same page. One day I said to Geoffrey Norris, Tony's private-sector adviser, that some of the images of women on TV were not always helpful. I suggested that we urge programme makers and advertisers to include more images of women as leaders and decision-makers.

'Can't you think what the *Daily Mail* headline is going to be if we do this?'

'What do you mean?' I asked.

'It's going to say, "Labour call for more lesbians on TV."'

'But we're not talking about lesbians, just women who are bright and intelligent.' But I knew he was right. You have to recognize that papers such as the *Daily Mail* will always look for the negative, whatever the story.

Anyway, the report was very well received and got a lot of publicity. After it was published I spent a year travelling around the country, speaking about it at universities, conferences and union meetings. The government produced a response on what they agreed with and a year or so later we reconvened to see what had happened. Around a hundred employers, including Tesco, the Royal Mail, oil companies and police forces, signed up to become exemplar employers by looking for ways to make it easier for women to work and providing training programmes. Sadly, like so many good initiatives, it hit a brick wall, as the Women's Equality Unit, run by Angela Mason, didn't follow it up. I don't blame Angela for this. I think Ruth Kelly, the minister for women, was the reason. She wasn't particularly interested in the report and was frightened of her own shadow. I was deeply disappointed that all this hard work the commission had done wasn't given the kind of importance it deserved.

I will always remember the Women and Work Commission, not just for the good work it did, but because it might have saved my life. When suicide bombers struck in central London on 7 July 2005 two of their targets, Russell Square tube station and a double-decker bus in Tavistock Square, were either side of my studio flat in Bloomsbury. Had I not been sitting in a hotel in Richmond chairing a meeting of the Women and Work Commission, I might have been among those killed and injured on that dreadful day.

When I saw a vacancy advertised for the deputy chair of the newly created Equality and Human Rights Commission in 2006, I applied for it. I was successful, probably because of my work in the past with the Equal Opportunities Commission. This new organization—a quango—was set up to replace the Commission for Racial Equality, the Equal Opportunities Commission and the Disability Rights Commission. Chaired by Trevor Phillips, the former chair of the Commission for Racial Equality, it would cover race, sexuality, religion and belief, age, and human rights. Such a broad remit meant that there wasn't a single person in the country not touched by the work of the commission. It occupied half of the second floor of the modern Norton Rose building near Tower Bridge and employed around 500 staff in London, Manchester, Cardiff and Glasgow.

It's common for a new organization to have teething problems, especially if, like the Equality and Human Rights Commission, it is bringing three bodies together; but I wasn't prepared for the kind of problems that I encountered in the commission's first year or so. The chief executive was Nicola

Brewer, a former senior civil servant from the Foreign and Commonwealth Office. She was very able, but out of her depth at the commission, where she had to set up systems and work with stakeholders. It took ages for proper finance, personnel and other systems to be put in place, which got us into big trouble. When the accounts were presented to parliament the auditor refused to sign them off because of irregularities. For example, the legal and strategic grants programme hadn't been properly accounted for and the staffing levels had exceeded the agreed number, which somehow nobody noticed.

As well as all this, rather than focusing on the commission as a whole, most of the board members, who were all appointed by Ruth Kelly, saw themselves as being there to campaign on behalf of their particular interest group, such as the disabled, gays and lesbians, or older people. And I always felt that Bert Massey, who had been the chair of the Disability Rights Commission, was miffed that he didn't have my job.

Jane Campbell, who was a big disability campaigner, and I once got into a fierce argument about abortion. There was some challenge in parliament to the Abortion Act, as there seems to be every year. She said that if a woman discovers that her foetus has a disability, she shouldn't have the choice to have an abortion.

'Well, why is it that we argue that women have the choice to abort perfectly healthy foetuses but can't have that choice if the foetus has a disability?'

Some of the board didn't think Trevor was suitable to be chair, and they tried to undermine him. And I didn't get on at all with Francesca Klug, the human rights academic. I couldn't be doing with the lack of straight talking that seemed to prevail, although I appreciated her knowledge in the field of human rights. I think both Trevor and I wondered what on earth we had got ourselves into.

Eventually, new board members were appointed, including Stephen Alambritis, former head of public affairs at the Federation of Small Businesses and now leader of Merton council; Jean Irvine, former head of HR at Post Office Ltd; and Ann Beynon, director of BT in Wales—and the commission got sorted out. I get on very well with Trevor, who is very charming and has a good sense of humour. He's what you might call a blue-sky thinker, full of ideas, whereas I'm more practical. When he comes up with an idea, I'll usually say, 'So how do we do that, then?'

One of the streams of work I've been particularly involved in is called Working Better, which has looked at a variety of issues, including opportunities for parents with families to work. We recommended that men and women could share paternity or maternity leave. We've produced reports on opportunities for disabled people in the workplace and in 2011 we published *Hidden in Plain Sight*, an inquiry into disability harassment.

We also looked into opportunities for older workers and those who had retired. We found that British Gas, for example, often took on people in their fifties as trainee engineers, and B&Q actively recruited retired people. I later launched a report at Tate Modern on the employment of older workers.

I know some people don't think much of quangos, seeing them as unnecessary and a waste of public money. I'll admit that in the early days of the commission we produced reports on subjects such as the care system or school leavers, and they ended up as meaningless because we had no plan of action to follow up on them. But we are well organized nowadays and, I believe, playing a valuable role in trying to create the kind of society where everyone is given the same chance. It might sound idealistic. But then, I think we all should have ideals about the kind of society we want to live in. We have statutory duties to ensure that public bodies are operating in a fair and transparent way.

I sat on the honours board of the Government Equality Office. The way it works is that we are given information about a person and asked to decide if he or she has done outstanding work in promoting equality and deserves to be nominated for an honour. MBEs are awarded to people who have done work at a local level, OBEs are given for work nationally and CBEs might include international work. Then there are also DBEs and KBEs. If we nominate someone who works in a school, for example, the Department for Education will then be asked for its opinion. This board has since been subsumed into the Home Office honours board, so I'm not sure how much emphasis is now placed on equality.

The board was not meant to be political, but if someone had spoken against the Prime Minister, we might decide not to put them forward. This would be true whoever was in office. It's about tact and diplomacy. Most of our nominations were accepted. For example, in 2011 we had eight of our eleven nominations accepted.

I once had a big row with one committee member over the nomination of Janet Veitch, who had been director of the Women's National Commission when I was its chair. During her holidays Janet ran equality courses for police forces and she was a member of the Women's Budget Group, which analyzes the government's budget for its effects on women. After leaving the Women's National Commission she worked for the Equality and Diversity Forum and did a lot of work in bringing young women interns forward. I thought she was a prime candidate. But one of the other members argued that she hadn't done anything outside her job. I knew that the real reason for this was personal. I thought it was very unprofessional.

Very few people know how the honours system works— but the civil servants do—and many of them get honours for simply doing their job. I think this is wrong. If we are going to award honours, then they should only go to people who have done something remarkable in their lives, not to people who just do their job. I can think of many women I met during my time at the T&G who were far more deserving of an award. The fact is that there are many women in the trade-union movement who, despite the pressures of family life and despite being in low-paid jobs, still volunteer to be shop stewards or health and safety officers, or spend time campaigning on issues such as pensions or flexible working for those with young children. In my book, they are far more deserving of an award than many of those who end up on the list.

14. You've Got Mail

AS A UNION OFFICIAL, my main focus in industrial relations had been trying to improve pay and conditions for the workers, especially women. I had never been involved in running a business. Although I'd always tried to look at industrial relations from both sides, you can never fully understand how someone else sees something until you stand in their shoes. I was about to enter the business world for the first time. It happened in 2004 when I received a phone call one morning from an executive recruitment company, or what are commonly known as headhunters.

'We've been asked to recruit someone for the board of the Royal Mail,' said a man's voice at the other end of the phone.

'The Royal Mail board? Oh,' I said, wondering if I had heard him correctly.

'Is this something that you might be interested in?'

'Er, yes,' I found myself saying, even though I hadn't really taken in what he said.

After completing the application form he sent me, I was called to an interview at a smart building in Mayfair. As I walked into the elegant and airy reception, I thought to myself, this company must make a lot of money. I felt very anxious. It wasn't just that I hadn't been to an interview in years, it was that, while I'd sat on lots of committees, and I was now a member of the House of Lords, I had no experience of sitting on a high-powered board. The interview turned out to be very informal. It was more of a chat. I discovered that the company had spoken to some officials in the DTI about me. I was quite well known in some circles at the DTI, as I had sat on the Fair Markets Board. Making my way back to Green Park tube station, I wondered how well I'd done.

But I must have done all right, because a couple of weeks later I was called to an interview at the Royal Mail head office in Old Street. Sitting in leather armchairs in front of me were Alan Leighton, the chairman; David Fish, chair of the remuneration committee, which set salaries and bonuses and pensions for the senior executives; Richard Handover, chair of the nominations committee; and Jonathan Evans, the company secretary.

'What do you think about the direction the Royal Mail is going?' asked Alan Leighton.

'Well, I can see that it's facing some big questions about how it adapts to the latest technology.'

'Yes. We're facing some serious issues, that's for sure,' he grinned.

'What do you think about the union?' asked David Fish.

'From what I've read, I think some of the things they do are a bit barmy.'

'Interesting...,' murmured Alan, scribbling on his notepad.

'One of the big problems with it is that no one at the top of the union has worked anywhere else apart from the Royal Mail,' I said.

'Yes, that's true,' said Alan.

'The officials have no experience of how other companies work, so they can't bring much to the negotiating table.'

When I left, I thought to myself, 'I'm not sure I have the right kind of technical knowledge for this sort of post.' Sitting on union committees is one thing, but sitting on the board of a company such as Royal Mail is another. Yet I liked the idea of using all the knowledge and experience I had gained to try and improve industrial relations at Royal Mail.

In September, I went to the Labour Party conference in Brighton. At the gala dinner, I was talking to a friend when I spotted the tall figure of Alan Leighton chatting to someone near the bar, so I decided to ask him if he had heard whether or not I would be appointed to the board. I knew that these sorts of appointments took a long time to make, not least because they had to be approved by the secretary of state. And parliament was in recess because it was the summer.

'How you doing, Alan?' I said.

'Hello!' he smiled and then he said, 'So you're going to come and join us, then?'

'Oh, you've heard?'

'Well she loves you, doesn't she?'

I knew he was referring to Patricia Hewitt, the secretary of state for trade and industry, who had responsibility for the Royal Mail. I later learnt that Patricia had pointed out to the board that there was no one sitting on it who understood industrial relations and how trade unions or Whitehall worked. I had first met Patricia when she worked with Harriet Harman at Liberty. When I sat on the Labour Party NEC I got to know her very well. I tried not to look too excited.

I made my way back across the crowded floor to my friend, my face beaming. 'I'm in,' I said.

Later, I learnt that I had been given the job ahead of Brenda Dean, the former general secretary of SOGAT, the print workers' union. Out of all the applicants, we had been the two shortlisted. I suspect I was chosen because I had a more varied union background.

In October I attended my first board meeting. Looking around at the other non-executive directors, I realized I was the only woman. Seated around the table with me were some of the biggest names in British business. Alan Leighton, the chairman, was also chairman of BHS and former chief executive of Asda; Adam Crozier, the chief executive, had been head of the Football Association; Richard Handover was the former chief executive of W. H. Smith; David Fish was chairman of United Biscuits Group and chairman of Christian Salvesen; Bob Wigley was Chairman of Merrill Lynch's European Corporate Banking Business; John Neil was the chief executive of the Unipart Group; and Mike Hodgkinson was the former chief executive of BAA.

Royal Mail is technically Royal Mail Holdings PLC, and is divided into four parts: Royal Mail Letters; Parcelforce Worldwide; GLS, a European parcel service; and Post Office Ltd. Back then, Royal Mail employed 198,000 staff and operated 14,500 post offices. Because of what is called the universal service, it has a statutory duty to deliver mail to every one of the 27 million addresses in the UK.

When Alan Leighton and Adam Crozier had arrived at the Royal Mail it was losing £1m a day, largely because of the decrease in the number of letters sent, as a result of more of us paying our bills and shopping on the internet. They turned it around by reducing staff and changing some of the practices, and at one point it was making money. If it was going to survive, then it had to modernize—something to which the union was resistant.

Its programme of closing post offices in some parts of the country had caused a big political row, but the fact was that in some rural areas there would only be a handful of customers a week. Originally many post offices relied on people coming in for benefits payments, car tax or TV licences. But as a result of benefit being paid direct into bank accounts, and more and more people paying car tax and TV licences online, business went down.

As part of my induction, I visited sorting offices, mail centres and post offices. What shocked me about the sorting offices was how scruffy they were. In factories health and safety are taken very seriously, but in the sorting offices little attention seemed to have been paid. When I was taken round Mount Pleasant—or 'Mount Unpleasant', as it's known by the unions—in Clerkenwell, once said to be the largest sorting office in the world, I couldn't believe what a dump it was. There were bags of post left lying around in the corridors and aisles, and the escalator didn't work. When I had attended national meetings of the partnership set up by Tom Sawyer at Rathbone Place, the head office of Letters, I pointed out to the management that the entrance to the building was a complete disgrace. It was very shabby.

I also visited a number of small post offices, including the one in Marchmont Street, Bloomsbury, around the corner from my studio flat, and I was shown the computer system they used.

When one of the board compared post offices to building societies, I said, 'Well, if we are going to do that, then someone needs to get the broom out.'

'What do you mean?' asked Alan.

'Most of them are so untidy, with bits of paper all over the place,' I said.

He laughed. But he knew what I meant.

I don't like the cold. So when I was asked to go out with a postie on what's called a 'walk', it was in the middle of winter, so I said, 'Shall we wait for the spring?'

Every Saturday morning before the monthly board meeting, the agenda and background papers would arrive by special delivery at my home in Hove. I had bought a flat there in an art deco block a few minutes from the sea in October 2003. It was hard work having to read all the various documents, especially the financial ones. Even though I had been treasurer of the Labour Party for five years, I still found it a struggle to understand lots of rows of figures.

It took me a long time to learn how to understand the financial reports. When I had sat on the Low Pay Commission, Adair Turner would look at the figures and understand them immediately. It would take me ages. I remember saying to my granddaughter Hannah, who is studying business, 'Do finance. Because if you can do numbers you'll go upwards.'

I attended a three-day course at the Institute of Directors to help me understand finance. We were split into groups.

I remember my group had to work out some figures for something or other. As everyone else reached for the calculators, I said, 'That will be £11,450.'

Everyone turned and looked at me.

I said, 'I'm completely useless with complicated accounts, but I can do mental arithmetic.'

Poking around sorting offices, mail centres and post offices gave me an insight into how the Royal Mail worked. But at the first few board meetings I said very little. I didn't understand what they were talking about half the time. But I couldn't find the courage to say this. I felt I was out of my depth and wondered if it had been a mistake to think that I could be part of a board with such experienced and knowledgeable figures from industry on it. I felt like a fish out of water. On the other hand, I reminded myself that I had a better grasp of what was involved in industrial relations, and a better feel for the workers, than anyone else on the board.

While several members had run multinational companies, they didn't seem to have had much contact with the workers on the shop floor. It became clear to me that the board was not as good as the union when it came to getting their point across to politicians and the media. They didn't seem to think this was important. I also knew more about how the political process worked in reality.

John Neil and Mike Hodgkinson didn't think much of trade unions. Both had worked at British Leyland during the strikes that crippled the company.

'I wasn't in the union when you were at British Leyland, but from what I can see of the vehicle-building industry you're looking at it through rose–tinted spectacles,' I said.

'What do you mean?' asked John.

'You think management was wonderful there, but it wasn't. It was very poor.'

'Really?'

'Yes. When the Japanese began making cars in the UK, why do you think they kept the British workforce but brought their own management?'

This isn't to say that I supported the car workers all the time. When I used to see TV images of a car park at Leyland full of workers with their hands raised and someone shouting through a megaphone, I used to think it looked a bit like mass hysteria.

At our fourth board meeting, which was held at the directors' dining room at Selfridges, Bob Wigley, who was appointed to the board of the Bank of England soon after, turned to me and said. 'When they decided they wanted someone like you on the board I was very much against it. I couldn't see the point of it.'

'Really?' I said. This was the last thing I expected to hear.

'But now I can,' he continued.

'You can?'

'Yes, you bring to the board something none of us have.'

When I heard this, I inwardly breathed a sigh of relief. I had been feeling so unsure of myself that I had been beginning to wonder whether I should continue sitting on the board.

The more meetings I attended the more I realized that many of the members didn't understand the way politics and government worked. Just as when I sat on the Labour Party NEC, I realized that no matter how important someone might seem, they didn't always get everything right.

When we were having discussions with the Treasury to try to persuade it to give us more money. I said, 'There's no point going on about Gordon. He's not going to give us money at the moment.'

'What do you mean?' asked Alan.

'He's focused on becoming the next Prime Minister. So he's not going to do anything that might draw public criticism.'

'Well, that's not logical,' said Adam.

'Well, since when was politics logical? It isn't. You have to think outside the box.'

No one on the board could see that politicians wouldn't do something that might be bad for them. They didn't understand that politicians usually think of their own interests first and the wider world second.

But I was impressed by the way they handled the often complex day-to-day issues in the Royal Mail. They made sure they knew their stuff every time they sat down in the board room. They weren't into long meetings that went round in circles and they liked everything concisely presented. If it wouldn't go on two sides of A4, then forget it.

Alan Leighton was one of the most charismatic people I've ever met. He could charm the birds off the trees. At meetings he had a habit of going around each of us to find out what we thought of something. If he didn't think much of it he'd say, 'It isn't worth diddly squat.' If he liked something, he'd often say, 'Big tick.' He was very amusing.

Postcomm, the regulator at the time, required Royal Mail to ensure that a certain percentage of letters posted First Class must arrive the following day. At board meetings we would be presented with charts containing all this information. It was very important to meet targets, especially as they affected the bonuses paid to the directors. If the targets weren't met, then their bonuses were reduced. We were always having discussions about how to generate more income and cut costs. Some on the board argued that anyone who didn't include their postcode should be charged more, as these letters had to be sorted by hand. I didn't agree with this.

As board members we each received a stipend, but we didn't live it up on expenses. If we went out to eat, Alan nearly always paid the bill himself. Each member was very conscious that, because they were sitting on the board of a public company, they had to do everything by the book.

Sometimes we went on away days to Penny Hill Park, a luxury country house and spa deep in the Surrey countryside. The away days were designed to help us think through future strategies. Often we would invite senior managers from different sections of the company to talk to us about the particular issues they were facing.

At one away day, Postcomm did a presentation. I could see that the board of the Royal Mail and the board of Postcomm didn't get on well. The chair of Postcomm adopted a very offhand attitude when he spoke. And he seemed to be implying that we didn't have a grip on things. This really got up the nose of Bob Wigley, who was chair of audit and risk. He looked as if he might explode at any minute. Afterwards, Bob brought in a company to go over our security procedures to make sure they were working properly. They were.

It didn't take me long to realize why the board needed someone who understood the way trade unions worked. Relations between the board and the unions were, for the most part, pretty poor. The board often said that the Royal Mail's greatest asset was its workers. I always replied that they had to start behaving as if they believed this. The fact is that the Royal Mail had never had a history of engagement with the workforce. Royal Mail employees were members of the Communication Workers' Union (CWU). It's an odd union. Half of it is responsible for Royal Mail and half for British Telecom and other communication companies, because it was created by a merger in 1995 of the Union of Communication Workers and the National Communications Union.

I said to Dave Ward, the CWU deputy general secretary and Royal Mail negotiator, 'Have you ever thought of introducing the question of annual hours into negotiations?'

Annual hours meant that each year you have to work a certain number of hours. You might work only a few hours a week during one part of the year but a lot of hours during the other part of the year. You received the same pay each month. This was the practice at British Sugar, for example, where I had helped to negotiate an annual hours contract, which reduced overtime but still proved popular with the workers. Employees worked a lot of hours in the summer when the sugar beet was being harvested but fewer hours in the winter, which gave them more time at home.

When Dave Ward admitted to me that he'd never heard of annual hours, I was absolutely astonished. It was such a basic practice in industrial relations. In fact, I would go as far to say that industrial relations at the Royal Mail were a throwback to the 1970s when unions and management were always at loggerheads. When I spoke with the national executive of the Communication Workers' Union, I was amazed how much in the dark ages they were. They told me that they were opposed to part-time work.

'Part-time work now a fact of life,' I said. 'What's important is to make sure part-time workers get a good deal.'

'We never had any women working in the sorting offices until the Sex Discrimination Act came into force,' said one of the executives, as if it was such a terrible thing. Even though it had happened thirty or so years ago, he still hadn't got used to it!

I remember speaking to a young woman with a family who worked for the Post Office in Sussex and her explaining that she couldn't get a holiday on the rota in the summer because she was too far down the list, as she hadn't been employed long enough. I thought it was wrong that management allowed this situation to continue.

I was amazed to discover that 'job and finish' was still in operation. This referred to a postman or woman going home after finishing their round. This practice had been common in the public sector at one time. But the unions had negotiated a deal with the workers, in other words they were given a payment if they accepted it being abolished.

One of the problems at Royal Mail was that management had allowed a culture of complacency to set in and the customer was not being put first. The workers thought their jobs would always be safe, as the Royal Mail was a public company.

For years the practice was that when a management position at a sorting office came up the person who had been employed there the longest would get the job. It didn't matter whether or not they had the skills or aptitude necessary for the job. They wouldn't receive any training or support, but were just left to get on with it. This led to the Royal Mail getting a reputation for bullying and bad behaviour among its first level managers. Because the number one priority for the managers of sorting offices and mail centres was to get the post out of the door every day, I think that they didn't think much about people issues.

Although my responsibility was to the board, not the union, I felt I could be helpful to the union by explaining to the board why it was doing certain things and why it was unhappy with something. When the union staged a series of strikes in 2007 over modernization plans, I acted as a kind of bridge. The board wanted to end job and finish, introduce new machinery and different shift patterns, and increase part-time work.

I suggested to Adam Crozier and the head of HR that the TUC should be asked to help resolve the dispute. They were all for this. I went to see Brendan Barber and we opened up some new discussions with the union.

Adam's argument was always that he wanted people to work the hours they were paid for. From the union's point of view this was hard to sell to the members, as many of them had second jobs and longer shifts would affect these. I didn't speak to the TUC throughout this process as the negotiations were the responsibility of management, but I did speak regularly to the union, who saw me as a link. And

I tried to persuade them that change had to happen. In the end, they accepted this, although that was much more Brendan's doing than mine.

During my time on the board, I learnt a few things I didn't know before about the postal service. For example, if a person's handwriting on a letter can't be read it's sent to a centre in Belfast which employs students to try and decipher it and work out its destination. And there's a committee that decides on which images should be used on stamps. At the beginning of the year it sends out a list of possible images.

In October 2008 at the Atrium restaurant in Millbank Tower I helped launch a commemorative edition of stamps to celebrate the contributions made to women's rights by six figures of the twentieth century: Barbara Castle; Marie Stopes; Claudia Jones; Eleanor Rathbone; and the sisters Millicent Garrett Fawcett and Elizabeth Garrett Anderson. Nicola Horlick, the so-called Superwoman of the City, also spoke, seeming to ramble on for ages.

I always like to share my experience and knowledge, so I was delighted to be asked to act as a mentor to a young woman in the HR department at Post Office Ltd. She was very experienced in human resources, having worked for several large companies, but knew little about dealing with trade unions. We met regularly to discuss various issues, and I would try to get her to look at things from the point of view of a trade union.

When I left the Royal Mail board in 2010 after six years, a lot of progress had been made in making the company better able to handle future challenges. The union, having recognized that the world had changed and that many of us rarely wrote letters now, had signed a modernization agreement and had accepted the closure of some mail centres and the introduction of new 'walk sort' machinery in some sorting offices. And there's now a modern and smart centre at Gatwick Airport, where letters are sorted by machinery into walk sequencing, in other words following the walk, or beat, of individual postmen and women. The management introduced a programme called World Class Mail, based on a business philosophy from Japan. The workers are seen as part of the solution, so they are asked for their opinions on how things should be done. This is the sensible way to run a business.

The Royal Mail has a difficult future ahead. Whichever way you look at it, you aren't going to get more people writing letters. The coalition government has decided to put it up for sale, although post offices will remain in public hands. But who will want to buy it? I believe the state should subsidise it, as it plays an important part in local communities. Although many people now use the internet for paying bills and communication, we shouldn't forget that a lot of older people don't.

I thoroughly enjoyed my time on the board. And I'm pleased to say that when I left there were three other women on it. I learnt a lot from the other board members. What distinguished them from many of the trade-union officials I'd worked with was that they didn't have large egos and they were very professional.

I've always thought that people who have large egos are trying to cover up a vacuum. They are insecure. People who really know what they are talking about don't feel threatened by what others say. And several of the members did a lot of work with charities. Richard Handover, for example, was involved with Kids Company in Peckham. My perception of those who ran businesses changed. Mind you, they all knew how to make sure agreements included things such as bonuses and their own pension plan.

14. In the House

'HAVE YOU DECIDED?' asked the well-spoken man in the immaculate blue suit sitting behind his large desk in a dusty, brown office.

'Yes. I think so.'

'And?' he asked, raising his eyebrows.

'Er, Battersea.'

'Mm. Battersea,' he said, as if he had never heard of it. 'We have to think about this. It's very important.'

I watched as he began slowly thumbing through the pages of a huge book open on his desk. I thought to myself, if he says no to Battersea, I won't have a clue what to say.

After a while, he looked up, leaned back in his leather chair and said slowly, 'Yes... I think that will be all right.'

I smiled, thinking to myself, if only my mum and dad could see me now. They would be so proud. Mum had been wrong in believing that you shouldn't get above your station in life. But she had been right when she told me that I was no better or worse than anyone else. It tickled me to think that from now on I would be known as Baroness Prosser of Battersea. My friend Nita Clark, who is married to Tony Benn's eldest son, will become a viscountess when Tony dies. She once said to me, 'I'm not likely to use it going around the Co-op.' Nor would I, I thought.

It was May 2004 and I was sitting in the office of the Garter King of Arms in an old building across the river from St Paul's Cathedral. It was a dusty, dark place, lined with shelves of old books. The Garter King of Arms is the person who has to agree your title. When you become a life peer, you are expected to choose a place that you have some sort of connection with. I chose Battersea, because I was born there and my dad came from there.

When I had received a letter informing me that I was to be made a life peer, the words of Tony Blair at the end of the NEC meeting at the Labour Party conference in Blackpool in 2001 came back to me. 'We'll have to thank you properly.' Receiving the OBE had been marvellous, but becoming a peer was something else. It meant that I'd be able to play a part in shaping legislation and speak about those issues I really cared about. I was one of forty-six new peers announced. The others included two more of 'the Four Margarets', Margaret McDonagh and Margaret Wall. According to the *Daily Telegraph*, we were 'Tony's cronies'. These kinds of gibes in the Tory media have never concerned me. Tony had once said to me that he felt the media hated Labour. There was some truth in that.

After agreeing the title, I then had to speak to the administrative people at the Lords and agree the date I would enter. Before I did this I would have to meet with Black Rod, the Clerk of the Parliaments and Lord Falconer, the leader of the House and Lord Chancellor. I was quickly realizing that becoming a peer meant entering a world where traditions and protocols mattered.

The following week, I was given a tour of the Lords. I've always found the Houses of Parliament an incredibly beautiful building. As a child, every time I saw it from the top of the bus I remember thinking that it looked a very important place. What hit me as I was shown around was the splendour, the sense of history and the colour. I discovered that while the carpet in the House of Lords is red, in the House of Commons it's green.

I met with Charlie Falconer and the Clerk of the Parliaments, the most senior administrator of the Lords, who talked me through behaviour and use of language. He explained that you were not allowed to use the word 'you' when you were speaking in the chamber.

Then I was taken to see Black Rod in his office. Black Rod is the Queen's representative in the Lords and manages the building, even though he has no management experience, as he is always from a military background.

'I'd like to show you this video,' he said, bending down in front of the TV and fiddling with a remote control.

The face of the newspaper proprietor Conrad Black appeared on the screen. Alongside him was Margaret Thatcher, who was introducing him in the Lords. This surprised me, as Black was already being talked about as a scallywag and a scoundrel. Surely he shouldn't be used as an example.

'Are you going to continue using this video?' I asked.

He looked at me as if I was bonkers. 'What do you mean?'

'Well, I don't think Conrad Black is the kind of person you should be using to represent members of the Lords.'

I don't know if different clips are shown now, but I would hope so, as Black is in prison for fraud. I should have thought then how a person can be very clever and half daft at the same time. How come Black Rod didn't see that a film featuring Conrad Black was completely inappropriate?

I then met with the banqueting manager to discuss what arrangements I wanted for my guests.

I entered the House of Lords on 7 July. Arriving at the peers' entrance, I felt very nervous. After my conversation with the Clerk of the Parliaments, who was quite a fierce-looking figure, I was worried that I would end up doing or saying something I shouldn't.

When my family and friends arrived, we went to the peers' guest bar for a glass of champagne, which is the tradition for new members. Peggy, the head bartender, who is Spanish, came over to welcome me. 'You will have the best service in the house,' she said.

As she walked away, Derek, my son-in-law, said, 'She knows a good customer when she sees one. And she can recognize an ex-trade unionist.'

I laughed. The cheeky bugger!

The maître d' then led us to the dining room, where a long table had been set for us. Flowers and place cards had been placed on it.

The doorkeeper came in just before 1.00 p.m. and asked me and Anne Gibson and David Lea, my two introducers, to follow him, while my guests were taken up to the gallery. He led us to the robing room at the end of the Queen's Gallery, where I was handed a scarlet robe with an ermine collar, the traditional attire for peers. I was then taken to the Moses Room, along with John Maxton, a former Scottish MP who was also entering the Lords, and we had a rehearsal with the doorkeepers playing the parts of Black Rod and the Garter King of Arms.

When it was time for the real thing, I entered the chamber walking behind Black Rod and Anne, with Garter and David bringing up the rear. The chamber was packed, as questions would immediately follow the introductions. Glancing at all the faces of the peers sitting in the chamber I felt very self-conscious. What on earth am I doing here? Is this really happening, or am I dreaming? When I reached the reading table, the clerk then read out a long introduction. Following this, I had to swear allegiance to the Queen and all her heirs and then sign some papers. When Garter waved his stick, we all bowed and were then led out of the chamber, shaking hands with the Lord Chancellor. As I passed the woolsack, everyone in the benches called out, 'Hear! Hear!'

It was then time for the official photograph. Standing in front of a huge fireplace in my red robes I felt like Father Christmas after he came down the chimney. I was then given several red booklets and a red case with my insignia on it.

Afterwards I was asked to take a seat in the chamber among the Labour peers. I have to admit that sitting there and looking at all these distinguished people sitting around me gave me a thrill. I only had to sit there for a few minutes.

My family and friends then rejoined me for photos and we went back to the dining room for afternoon tea. As we were chatting, a bell sounded and Margaret Wall, who had been introduced the previous week, grabbed hold of me. 'Come on, Margaret.'

'What?'

'You have to vote.'

I got up from my seat, not having a clue of what I was supposed to do, and hurried after her down a long corridor to the voting lobby to vote with the 'not contents', as it was a Conservative amendment. I found it all a bit surreal.

I didn't know this then, but a desk in the Lords is like gold dust. Because of the lack of space in the building, some peers have to work in nearby offices. David and Anne had saved me a desk in their office on the first floor of the West Front. Through the window I could see Westminster Abbey. Diana Warwick, Len Fyfe, chairman of Unity Trust Bank, and Bob Sheldon, a former MP and treasury minister in the Wilson government, also had desks in the same office. John Monks later moved into the office after Diana moved out and, in 2011, after Lord Fyfe died, my best friend, Ray Collins, moved in. He had become general secretary of the Labour Party, but was now stepping down from this role.

Anita Gale, who had been secretary of the Labour Party in Wales, and whom I had got to know through the Women's National Commission, was appointed as my mentor to show me the ropes. And there was a lot to learn in those first few weeks. She told me where to get the daily running orders and stationery, where to post letters (there's a post office in the Commons lobby and a number of post boxes in the buildings), and where to get a cup of tea.

She also explained the rules of the chamber. I learnt that you are not allowed to stand while the speaker is standing and you are not allowed to speak in debates unless you are listed in the daily notes. However, you are allowed to interrupt a speaker, but only if you have an important point to make. You do this by standing up and then the person speaking sits down. You are not allowed to use the word 'you' when addressing another peer. This is very bad form. Members must be addressed as 'noble lords' or, if you are talking about your own benches, 'my noble friend'. At questions, if you want to ask a supplementary to someone else's question you have to stand up and hope to be heard. The speaker doesn't chair proceedings like the speaker of the Commons. The Lords is self-regulatory. Generally, interventions and questions go round the benches, so peers from each party get a chance to speak.

My pass gives me access to the whole Parliamentary Estate, so I can go into the Commons, although not into the chamber. Likewise MPs can come into the Lords, but not the chamber. We are not allowed to use each other's refreshment facilities unless accompanied. Someone told me this was to do with tax and the subsidies which operate in the Commons. The food is actually pretty variable. Formal meals in the Peers' Dining Room or Barry Room are usually very good, but meals in other more casual eateries are less so.

Most people would be surprised to know that the Health and Safety at Work Act doesn't apply in the Lords, because it's royal property. As a result there are mice scurrying around everywhere: in the dining room, the bishops' bar and the peers' guest bar. There are lots of traps all over the place and the rooms are vacuumed twice a day. What we need is a cat!

The Lords is a little bit like a club. Each time I walk through the peers' entrance and into the peers' lobby, I always think, 'Oh, my God, what am I doing here?'

Unlike the House of Commons, the House of Lords is not elected, of course. The government appoints them, like me, or they are hereditary members—in other words the aristocracy—or Anglican bishops. In 2012 there were 827 members of the Lords, over 700 of them life peers and nearly a quarter of them women.

I believe this mix gives the Lords a much broader range of knowledge and experience to draw upon than the House of Commons. We have people sitting in the Lords who have risen to the top in business, health, finance, science, law, the media, charities, you name it. As a Tory minister said to me, 'Answering questions is very nerve wracking, as they are all experts. Some have even got a bloody Nobel Prize in their subject!'

At least a dozen people I have worked closely with over the years are now members. Apart from Ray Collins, there is also Bill Morris, Anne Gibson, John Monks, Maggie Jones and, as I mentioned earlier, Margaret McDonagh and Margaret Wall.

Each day when you arrive at the Lords, you have to visit the printed paper office to pick up the order papers for the business of the day. Just before a debate starts, a sheet is printed with the names of all those who are going to speak and all the numbers of the amendments.

The most difficult thing I found in my first weeks was finding my way around the building. It's a maze of corridors and nooks and crannies. I've never had a great sense of direction at the best of times. I was given a coloured map of the different floors and I took it with me everywhere. One day, I got completely lost, so I went up to one of the doorkeepers and said, 'I seem to have lost the West Front.'

He smiled and said, 'Let me give you a hint, my lady. If you look down that way it's very light.'

'Yes?'

'That's the river. Look that way. It's darker.'

'Yes?'

'That's the road. So that's West Front.'

'Thank you.' I thought this was pretty sound advice.

I had to learn the correct protocol in the chamber. I soon discovered that the worst thing you could do was to stand up when the speaker stood up. If you did this, members would shout out, 'Order! Order!' If you are in the corridor when the speakers' procession comes past, you have to stand silently as a mark of respect for the office.

I found the first few weeks as a peer confusing. So much so that during a major vote, when I was looking for Ann Gibson, I wandered into the chamber, walking between the woolsack—the speakers' chair—and the big cushion where the whips sit. Suddenly everyone was shouting 'Order' and glaring at me. I stood there, not having a clue what I had done wrong, and feeling stupid. I was so confused that I turned around and walked back the same way. This time the shouting was even louder. I couldn't wait to get out. As I reached the door, I said to the doorkeeper, 'Oh my God, I need to get out of here!'

'I'm sorry, m'lady, the doors are locked.'

No one had told me that the doors are locked eight minutes after a vote begins.

The House sits at different times. On Monday and Tuesday we sit at 2.30 p.m., on Wednesday at 3.00 p.m., on Thursday at 11.00 a.m. and on Friday at 10.00 a.m. The house usually rises, as they say, at 10.00 p.m. Dinner is between 7.30 p.m. and 8.30 p.m. when what is known as Dinner Break Business, a debate, takes place.

The whips try to get all voting done by 7.30 p.m., before many peers, especially crossbenchers, go home. If you're involved in a debate or amendments, then you must be there from start to finish. It's considered bad manners when speaking not to be there to hear the speaker before and after you. But if you are speaking about an amendment, not a debate, you are not expected to stay until the end. The front door always remains open while the house is sitting.

Some days can be very long. For example, I might have to catch the train early in the morning from my home in Hove to Victoria, get a cab to Euston and then catch another train to Manchester for an Equality and Human Rights Commission meeting. When I get back to London, I might have to attend a vote in the House in the evening, so I wouldn't arrive home until after ten.

I don't spend a great deal of time in the chamber unless I am involved in a debate. As we have no secretarial help, there is always a lot of paperwork to do and, of course, I have to be up to speed with Equality and Human Rights Commission business. Sharing a small office with five other peers can mean things get a bit manic at times, what with phones ringing and people dashing in and out.

The most interesting part of the day is usually oral questions, which take place at the start of each session after prayers. Four questions are on the order paper and each one is allocated seven minutes. It's usually very lively: the opposition tries to put the minister on the spot but the government benches are sometimes quite sycophantic. The coalition government has some pretty poor ministers in the Lords who find it difficult to think on their feet and just read from the brief.

In an average week there will be days when the voting is important, so being in the building is very necessary. Coming together to vote is quite good as you catch up with people whom you might not otherwise see. We get a text service from the whips office, which alerts us when a vote is coming up.

When you become a peer people and organizations that want you to take up their issues lobby you. Every day you receive background papers about key issues. Most are sent by campaigning organizations and charities. For example, on one occasion, Voluntary Services Overseas asked me to ask a question about the new UN agency, UN Women. There's loads of stuff you are supposed to read, but it's not always possible. However, I always try and spend a few minutes reading the newsletter the Battersea Society send me each month.

At the heart of the Lords, of course, are the debates. Since becoming a peer, I've taken part in over twenty, mainly to do with issues such as the rights of women, employment, equality and diversity, the Post Office and international policy.

I've always believed that knowledge is power. And this is very true in the Lords. If you know how the rules work, you know how to use them. If you are taking part in a debate you need to prepare well, especially as some of the peers might have a great deal of knowledge about a particular subject. You don't want to appear a complete wally. I usually do this by searching for relevant papers in the Lords library and inviting organizations or individuals to provide me with a briefing. For example, in 2011 when I was preparing for the second reading of the Legal Aid Bill, I received briefings from the TUC, the Citizens Advice Bureau, various housing associations and the Law Centres Federation.

Every year on International Women's Day Joyce Gould, a senior member of the House and formerly a national organizer with the Labour Party, always puts down for a debate, and I've always participated in it. One year, I arrived back at Heathrow from a holiday in India and headed straight to the Lords so I wouldn't miss it. The debate in 2011 was particularly pleasing because all parties took part in it. Traditionally it's been Labour peers and a few Lib Dems who have taken part. This sends a bad message out about women from the Conservatives.

When I took part in the Postal Services Bill debate, I told the House that I thought privatization was inevitable and not necessarily a bad thing. There was a great need for a large financial injection. Other public bodies had been privatized with excellent results: British Telecom, for example. When the company was public it was chaotic. A friend of mine who worked for it said they didn't even know how much it cost to manufacture a phone. Since privatization, the service has been very good.

I was aware that this was the first time I'd spoken on behalf of employers, not workers, and predictably it landed me in hot water. Lord Tony Clarke, who had been on the national executive of the CWU, was fuming. When I came out of the chamber, he came up to me by the lift and said, 'I never thought I'd see the day when you joined the managers.'

'Well, unlike you Tony, I worked for a union that had to deal with all kinds of employers, big and small, public and private, and I had to learn to understand where they were coming from,' I replied. He had only ever worked for the Royal Mail, so knew nothing about the bigger picture where industrial relations were concerned. However, I was anxious about how privatization might affect the workforce. The thing that made me cross with the Communication Workers' Union was that during the period of the debate it should have been negotiating with management to make sure that clauses were included in the bill to protect the workers. Instead it did nothing except complain.

The secret to taking part in a debate is never to talk for longer than your allotted time, stick to the subject at hand, demonstrate that you know your stuff and, if possible, show a bit of humour. I remember a debate about moving the judges from the jurisdiction of the House of Lords to the Supreme Court across Parliament Square. When it turned to the facilities in the new building, the questions went on so long that I thought we might start talking about how many toilets they were going to have. When Charlie Falconer, who was Lord Chancellor at the time, told one ancient judge that he would have made a good shop steward for the T&G, the House broke into fits of laughter.

I once got annoyed with John Prescott, because he kept talking when the speaker stood up.

'Shut up!' I said, just loud enough for him to hear.

He leaned across and said, 'I'm surprised at you, love, a trade unionist, telling me about the constitution.'

When I saw him the next day I said, 'Have you got over your miseries?'

He just laughed.

I said, 'If you came from the north-west they would have said you had a cob on.'

Most members of the Lords will sit on at least one committee or sub-committee. I'm a member of sub-committee G, a sub-committee of the select committee on Europe. It consists of members from across the parties and meets on Thursday mornings. It is one of many committees that focus on issues in Europe. We discuss social policy and we have produced reports on topics such as grassroots sport, the movement of healthcare professionals around Europe and the European Social Fund. Our reports go to the main select committee to be signed off and then there is usually a debate on the floor of the House.

I'm also a voluntary member of four all-party groups: London, statistics, gender, and the sustainability and ethics of fashion. The groups regularly invite speakers from various bodies to inform us about key issues. The London group, for example, might invite representatives from organizations such as Transport for London, the Royal Opera House and the Olympic Park Authority to explain what they do. Statistics might seem an odd topic to discuss, but it's very important. If you can't back up your argument in a debate with statistics, then fighting your corner is more difficult. All-party groups are quite influential. If a letter from an all-party group is sent to an organization people tend to read it.

As well as this, I'm also a member of the Labour peers group, which meets every Wednesday at 5.00 p.m. Usually around fifty members attend. Our chief whip will run through forthcoming debates and the Labour leader of the Lords will report back on any meetings she has had and we will usually have a guest speaker.

Nowadays in parliament, of course, security is very tight. But when US President Barack Obama delivered an address in Westminster Hall in 2011 there were armed police patrolling everywhere. No one was allowed to bring a car into the car park and no guests were allowed other than partners. There was a very amusing moment when the woman who is head of the doorkeepers announced, 'And I must remind you all that when Mr Obama leaves you must not enter the aisles.' Ray and I were in hysterics. Did she think we were all going to rush up on to the stage? Obama began by noting that the only other people who had addressed both Houses were the Queen, Nelson Mandela and the Pope, then adding, 'This is either a very high bar or the start of a funny joke.' His speech wasn't earth-shattering, because he was addressing a cross-party audience, and didn't want to be too political, but he knew how to hold an audience.

Aside from all the debates and committee work, I spend a fair amount of time hosting receptions or entertaining guests. In 2011, for example, I held a reception for Warwick University to talk about how it has modernized the trade-union records office. I have also hosted a reception for a wonderful Afghan woman who talked about building and supporting schools for girls on the Afghanistan–Pakistan border. It's very dangerous work.

The trip I made to Chile in 1986 will always stay with me, not least because I had to run for my life to avoid being tear-gassed. So it was wonderful to take afternoon tea with Joan Hara when she was visiting London. She told me she was setting up a school in Chile in memory of her husband. 'I want him to be remembered as more than a poster on the wall,' she said.

There always seems to be talk about reforming the House of Lords. In 2012 the coalition government are trying to push through a bill to have all members of the Lords elected. This is Nick Clegg's idea. I think the bill is very poor. It suggests that representatives should be elected for a fifteen-year term and that there should be constituencies a similar size to the European parliament constituencies, which are huge. How this makes the process more democratic and accountable is beyond me. The bill reduces the opportunities for representatives to be close to their constituency. It suggests several methods of voting, including a party-list system, which is how the MEPs are elected. You would end up with a load of people who were in the Lords not because of their experience and expertise but because of their party affiliation.

I'm not against reform. I think we need more transparency about the way someone is appointed to the Lords and a greater spread to ensure that the Lord reflects ethnicity, disability and gender. I have to say that I don't agree with Anglican bishops sitting in the Lords. The bishops aren't allowed to vote, but they are very good at campaigning. If they take up an issue, they always manage to get Church members to write letters or send e-mails. Margaret Wall said to me one day, 'If you find yourself standing up when the Lord Speaker stands up, you can sit on a bishop's seat—or if there's no seat available sit on a bishop's lap.'

The money we receive for our work in the Lords is known as an allowance. Unlike MPs, we don't receive a salary. We can claim daily expenses, overnight expenses if our main homes are outside the M25, secretarial expenses and travel costs. In 2009 it was discovered that some peers had been claiming expenses for things they shouldn't have. There's no excuse for this, as the expenses form we complete is quite straightforward. You have to declare that you were in the House on a certain day and what you did, attending a debate in the chamber or voting, for example. It's pretty hard to make a mistake on the form.

My home is in Hove, although I own a studio flat in Bloomsbury, which I stay in during the week when I'm in London. But Hove is my main home. Anyone who claims a room or a tiny cottage as the main home when they have a big house in London is clearly stretching the truth. Some people seem to have got away with fiddling their expenses, as there was insufficient proof against them. Others have been banned from attending the House. If you get caught fiddling your expenses, then you have to face the consequences. As a result of the scandal, changes were made to the allowance system. We now claim one single daily amount whether or not we live in London. Those of us who live outside have had a 10 per cent reduction in our expenses.

Most peers I know felt angry about the revelations over expenses, as it makes the public think we are all at it. The fact is that there are many outstanding people in the Lords. One of the peers I admire most is Lord David Ramsbottom, who raises questions about the Prison Service and the Court Service time and time again. I also admire Lord Mawson, who runs a massive community programme in the East End and campaigns on behalf of ordinary working people. And some of the hereditary peers do excellent work. The Earl of Listowel, for example, speaks up for young people in care.

I've never been to university. But I now have two degrees, one from the University of East London and another from London Metropolitan University. The University of East London is the successor of the Polytechnic of North East London, where I studied all those years ago. It has a wonderful campus, much nicer than the place where I studied in Stratford. The university runs a programme for former students to make donations, which are used for research by different departments. In 2010 I presented the awards.

I love going into schools to talk to young people and listen to their views on politics and society. Hundreds of schools contact the Lords each year requesting guest speakers. The first time I did this was at a girls' school in Chislehurst in Kent. The pupils bombarded me with lots of questions, such as why we went to war in Iraq and why there were such high numbers of black people in prison.

'What was the most exciting moment in your career?' asked one girl.

I thought for a moment and then said, 'Well, I suppose shaking hands with Nelson Mandela.'

'Why has Boris Johnson introduced changes to children's bus passes?' asked another girl.

This question threw me. I didn't have a clue, so I said, 'I have to be honest and say I don't know.'

At the end of the talk several girls gathered around me. One of them said, 'Can we ask you a question?'

'Of course.'

'Where did you get your watch?'

'I bought it in New York.'

'OK. Thank you.' And off they went. I found this very amusing.

I enjoyed the visit and thought the girls seemed very bright. I returned to the school a few months later to present the annual prizes.

However, when I gave a talk at a college in Bexley it was a bit of a disaster. I stood on a stage in a packed hall, but the students were too far away, and I could sense them getting restless. When I invited questions, only a couple of them responded. I also got the impression that many of them didn't really want to be there.

At a comprehensive school in Southampton I was invited to, I was interviewed and filmed by a group of pupils taking part in a BBC schools media project. One of the pupils wanted to know what I thought about the Big Society. I told her that you couldn't just conjure up community activity out of thin air. It had to be built up. I said that the government believed local authorities should provide services for women suffering from domestic abuse, but the local authorities had to implement cuts, so they had no money.

I was pleased to see so much interest among children in politics. This is vital for our democracy. When children ask me why politicians seem out of touch with people, I reply that many have never been out there and done anything. If you study philosophy, politics and economics at university, then work for an MP or someone, and then become an MP yourself, you don't have much experience of the world and lack the common touch.

The Labour leader Ed Milliband is a good example of this. When he attended a fundraising party organized by Charlie Falconer for the Labour Party's Thousand Club, I thought he looked for all the world like a dummy in a shop window. He never moved a muscle the whole time Charlie spoke. He stood there, arms by his side, staring into middle distance. When Charlie finished his speech, everyone clapped, but Ed never even acknowledged it. It was bizarre. I can't understand why his PR advisers don't teach him to look at people instead of looking through them.

I've always believed that if you have any influence, then you should encourage and support young people. Since becoming a peer, I've tried to do this in whatever way I can, such as judging a design competition for a canvas bag at the University of London's School of Oriental and African Studies to raise money for the Terence Higgins Trust, and using my contacts to help an enterprising young man who had developed a website for graduate interns.

Much of my story has been about my attempts to create a society that is fair, in which both men and women have the same opportunities. Perhaps I've not always succeeded, but I've never given up. One thing I am convinced of is that it's always better to have tried and failed than to have never tried at all. And I hope I've done that.